MARKING THE MASSES

THOMAS J. HUGHES

MARKING THE MASSES
BY THOMAS J. HUGHES

© 2023 by Ingenuity Films.

Published by Ingenuity Films.
PO Box 727
New Smyrna Beach, FL 32170
www.IngenuityFilms.com

All rights reserved. No portion of this book may be reproduced, stored in a retrieval system, or transmitted in any form or by any means without prior written permission from the publisher.

ISBN: 979-8-218-22107-2

All Scripture quotations, unless otherwise indicated, are taken from the New King James Version®. Copyright © 1982 by Thomas Nelson, Inc. Used by permission. All rights reserved.

Cover created by Midjourney AI art tools. Licensed by Ingenuity films LLC for commercial use. Modified by Brent Miller Jr.

Printed in the United States of America

Contents

Introduction 1
Bel Air, Los Angeles – 1961 1
The Backyard Overlooking the World 4
A Master Plan 5

PART ONE — QUESTIONS AND ANSWERS

Chapter 1 — Things You Need to Know 9
Can the Impossible Become Inevitable? 10
Who is the Beast? 11
Who is the Dragon? 12
Who is the Second Beast? 12
Can the Mark of the Beast Be Understood at Face Value? 13

Chapter 2 — Beastly Deceptions 15
What is the Mark's Purpose? 15
Could Things Really Get that Bad? 17
How Will They Sell the Mark to the Public? 18
How Will God View the Mark? 18
Will People Receive the Mark by Trickery, Accident, or Deception? 19
What Will Happen to the Unmarked? 22
Does This Mean One-world Government? 23

Chapter 3 — Spire of Babel 25
How Could Nimrod Keep His One-World Government? 25
How Can a Disjointed World Unite? 27

PART TWO — FOLLOWING THE SCIENCE

Chapter 4 — Technology Shrinks the Earth **31**
The World in Your Living Room 32
Technology and the Promise of Peace 34
Industrialized Death 34

Chapter 5 — Science: The World's New Master **37**
Greta Thunberg 38
Climate Mania 40
Herbert George Wells and a New World Order 41
Science in Charge 42

Chapter 6 — Making Man in Our Own Image **45**
Men Like Gods 46
Technology Derails Evolution 47
Directed Evolution 48

Chapter 7 — People of the Abyss **49**
Sterilization of Failure 50
Eugenics Goes Mainstream 51
Kill, Kill, Kill, Kill, Kill 52
Ill-shaped and Ailing 54
Germany Follow the Science 54
Fixing the Abyssians 55
Wealth, Poverty, and Control 57

**Chapter 8 — "Intellects Vast and Cool
and Unsympathetic"** **59**
Technocrats In Control 60
Hollywood Weights In 61

Follow the Money 62
Enlightened Governance 63
The Man Who Was Science 63
Mom and Dad: The Masked Strangers 65

Chapter 9 — The Middleman for the Medicine Men 67
Turning Science into Doctrine 67
The Moral Decision 69
Do We Really Want to Put Science in Charge? 70

PART THREE — DISASTER AHEAD

Chapter 10 — Paradise Through Unity 75
Peace on Earth? 76
Truman and the Bomb 76
The Prophesied Fire of Destruction 78
Fear of Armageddon 79
One World or None 79
An End to National Sovereignty 80
Global Control of Individuals 82
Earth's Leadership Vacuum 84

Chapter 11 — The Problem with People 87
Cogs on Gears Within Sprockets Turning Wheels 88
Man Taking Charge of Man 89
The Global Authority 90
One Authoritative Source 91

Chapter 12 — The Open Conspiracy 95
A Federal Government of All Humankind 96
Swallowing Up the World 97
An End to Private Ownership 98
'Imagine No Possessions' 99
A Spoonful of Sugar 100
Kumbaya Without the Prayer 101
Teeth 103
World Federalist Movement 104
Democracy Acts Up… Again 105

PART FOUR — INSANITY BY DESIGN

Chapter 13 — The New Generations 109
The Kids 109
Nightmare Minds 111
Debased Minds 112
The Manchurian Children 114
Love and Hate 115
Troubled Minds… On Purpose 116

Chapter 14 — The Rise of Wokeism 119
The Power of Language 120
The Woke Family 121
Social Insanity 122
A New Religion 124
The Final Countdown 125
What About the Rapture 127

PART FIVE — VIRAL MANIPULATIONS

Chapter 15 — Could Vaccines Be the Mark of the Beast? 131
The Mark of the Beast Needs a Beast 132
Unrepentant and Unforgiven 133
The Angel's Global Proclamation 134
Receiving the Mark Involves the Worship
of Antichrist and of Satan 135
Penalties Will Be More Extreme 136
A Couple of Other Differences… 137

Chapter 16 — What Vaccine Mandates Teach Us 139
Beware of Government Empowering Itself 139
The Rallying Cry of the Tyrant 141
Financial Life or Death 141
Eyes Everywhere 142
"It Was About Compliance" 142
Arrests 144
The Money Bomb 145

Chapter 17 — Crushing Human Rights 147
Child Abuse? 147
Human Rights Give Way to Government Power 148
Oceans of Propaganda 149
'These Aren't the Droids You're Looking For' 151
Fake News and Free Speech 153
The DHS's 'Disinformation Governance Board' 154
Real Motives 157

PART SIX — BEAST WORLD

Chapter 18 — The Beast System 161
What Does "666" Mean? 161
Why the Hand or Forehead? 162
What Will the Physical Mark Be? 163
Will the Mark Be Visible? 164
An Implanted Chip? 165
In or On? 166

Chapter 19 — Brave New Possibilities 167
The Brain-Computer Interface 168
Knowledge Rentals 169
Scary Outcomes 170

Chapter 20 — The Beast's Reign 173
How Do We Know Antichrist's Government
Will be Totalitarian? 173
How Bad Could It Be? 174
Could Dissenters Hide? 175
When Can Such Technology Can Be Built? 176
Starlink and the New Constellations 177

Chapter 21 — Beast Money 179
What Will Happen to Cash? 179
What Will Replace Cash? 180
One Money, One World 182

Chapter 22 — Why People Allow Government to Domination **185**
Reason #1 - Peace and Safety 185
Reason #2 - Convenience and Ease 187
Reason #3 - Financial Rescue and the Promise
of Prosperity 189

Chapter 23 — Super Capacities **191**
How Can So Much Data Be Stored? 192
How Can Anyone Make Sense of So Much Data? 194
ChatGPT 196
The Creation Becomes the Creator 197
Marking the Masses 198
The Image of the Beast 199
Growing Deception 200
Always Watching 201

PART SEVEN — HOPE AND VICTORY

Chapter 24 — Tipping Point **205**
Can the Horrors of the Mark Be Avoided? 207
Should Christians Be Concerned? 208
How Can I Be Sure I Am Ready? 209

Introduction

Bel Air, Los Angeles – 1961

The house glowed golden against the dark night. The air gently vibrated with mellow music and quiet conversation, punctuated by soft eruptions of laughter. It was not a raucous party, nothing for the neighbors to complain about.

But the currents of history flowed into and through that quiet dinner party. Amazing people filled the house, people intent on turning history's page from the past to the future. They were 20th century men molding the 21st century world.

Even the home would become legendary. Henry Singleton had commissioned famed architect Richard Neutra to design it, and it had been completed in 1959. Located on Mulholland Drive, in the Bel Air section of Los Angeles, today it is known as the "Singleton House."

Like Henry Singleton, most of his guests that night were associated with a newly-formed company called Teledyne. Singleton co-founded Teledyne in 1960. He would serve as CEO until

1986 and as Board Chairman until 1991. George Kozmetsky, the other co-founder, was also present at the party that night. Another Board member present was Arthur Rock. Singleton and Kozmetsky formed Teledyne with a $450,000 investment from Rock. He would later make key, early investments in Intel and Apple.

A fourth Board member was also present that night — Claude Shannon. You may never have heard of Shannon, but every minute of every day his ideas influence your life. He is known as the "father of information theory." Jimmy Soni and Rob Goodman wrote a book whose title explains Shannon's importance — *A Mind at Play: How Claude Shannon Invented the Information Age.*[1]

In 2016, The New Yorker ran an article commemorating what would have been Shannon's 100th birthday. In it, science writer James Gleick said, "Einstein looms large, and rightly so. But we're not living in the relativity age, we're living in the information age. It's Shannon whose fingerprints are on every electronic device we own, every computer screen we gaze into, every means of digital communication. He's one of these people who so transform the world that, after the transformation, the old world is forgotten."

The Prologue of Gleick's book, *The Information: A History, A Theory, A Flood*, begins with a Shannon quote. Then it says, "After 1948, which was the crucial year, people thought they could see the clear purpose that inspired Claude Shannon's work, but that was hindsight."[2]

---

[1] A Mind at Play: How Claude Shannon Invented the Information Age by Jimmy Soni and Rob Goodman, Simon & Schuster, 2017.

[2] The Information: A History, A Theory, A Flood by James Gleick, Pantheon Books, 2011.

INTRODUCTION

Gleick then spoke of two world-changing things — an object and an idea — that emerged from Bell Telephone Laboratories that "crucial year." One was a monograph written by Shannon called, "A Mathematical Theory of Communication." He soon published it in book form, appropriately renamed, *The Mathematical Theory of Communication*. The monograph introduced the term "bit" as a measurement of information. It helped science to see information as something measurable — a product, a commodity, and not insubstantial.

The other thing that came out of Bell Labs at that time was the transistor,[3] the small semiconductor that makes modern electronics physically possible. Historians credit three men with the invention. They later received the Nobel Prize for their work. One of them, William Shockley, was also at the party that night.

After helping to invent the transistor, unlike his co-inventors, Shockley went to work perfecting it. He started Shockley Semiconductor Laboratory in 1956. He placed it in the Mountain View/Palo Alto area of California because Palo Alto was his hometown, and he wanted his company to be near his elderly mother. Shockley Semiconductor Laboratory was the first establishment working on silicon semiconductors in what we now call Silicon Valley. Members of his team went on to found some of the most famous and influential companies in history. He is

---

[3] On December 23, 1947, William Shockley, John Bardeen, and Walter Brattain were able to demonstrate transistor amplification. Most reference works consider that the date of the transistor's invention. Gleick referenced 1948 because that was the year Bell Labs announced the invention and probably because that was the year Shockley invented the bipolar junction transistor (BJT), for the first time using a silicon base, and opening the door for actual commercial use of transistors. In the October 11, 2019 issue of ElectronicDesign, Lou Frenzel wrote, "The invention of the bipolar junction transistor [in 1948] was the milestone that kicked off the semiconductor industries."

known as "the man who brought silicon to Silicon Valley."

Later in life he became an open advocate of eugenics.

There were others there that night whose names you will not find in history books, but many of them also played roles in inventing the future. One of them was my dad, Jim Hughes. At age thirty, he was one of many present that evening — including Singleton and Kozmetsky — who had come from Litton Industries.

Through the years, I had heard my dad mention the Bel Air party. One part of his story particularly fascinated me. So, in March of 2022, I recorded a conversation with him, by then in his nineties. I asked him to tell me again what he remembered about that party. He told about some of the individuals there that night and their historical importance. Then came the intriguing part.

The Backyard Overlooking the World

A night drive along Mulholland Drive in Los Angeles offers breathtaking vistas. On one side, a traveler sees the vast San Fernando Valley with iconic film studios. On the other side, he can gaze out on the Los Angeles basin.

The Singleton House sits on the basin or south side of the road. Its backyard overlooks a vast portion of the Los Angeles area including Beverly Hills and downtown. On a clear night, the view extends beyond Los Angeles into Long Beach and into Orange County cities such as Anaheim, Santa Ana, Huntington Beach, and Irvine. By 1961, millions of people lived within the view of that backyard.

At the party, my father and several other men stepped into the yard to take in the view. They looked out at the lights that seemed to go on forever, and they chatted. Then one of them said, "Someday, we're gonna control all of the people that you see out there."

More than sixty years later, my nonagenarian father clearly remembers the statement, but he's not certain who said it. He thinks it might have been Claude Shannon, the father of information theory. But he doesn't know. Neither is he sure what the statement meant. Still, as he told me in 2022, "It really struck me and stuck with me all of my life."

A Master Plan

Most prophecy students agree with James Gleick's statement, "1948… was the crucial year." But we have different reasons. He said it because the information age was built on Shannon's 1948 work and because the transistor made its entrance into the world possible.

In Bible prophecy, 1948 is also the crucial year. In that year, God fulfilled His ancient promise to give Israel a national rebirth. It is the prophecy that gives meaning to all the signs of the times. It is the prophetic sign that makes everything else fit. And it is as unlikely, and therefore as much of a miracle, as the parting of the Red Sea.

Today, for the first time in history, humans are gaining the ability to make possible the literal fulfillment of Bible prophecy regarding the Mark of the Beast. My dad's story made me realize that the intellectual and technical innovations of the information age burst onto the world scene the same year Israel did.

And with the information age still in infancy, my own father heard one of its inventors make the prophetically jaw-dropping statement, "Someday, we're gonna control all of the people that you see out there."

PART ONE

Questions and Answers

MARKING THE MASSES

PART ONE: QUESTIONS AND ANSWERS

CHAPTER 1

Things You Need to Know

He causes all, both small and great, rich and poor, free and slave, to receive a mark on their right hand or on their foreheads, and that no one may buy or sell except one who has the mark or the name of the beast, or the number of his name. Here is wisdom. Let him who has understanding calculate the number of the beast, for it is the number of a man: His number is 666.
— Revelation 13:1618

The Apostle John placed those words on parchment near the end of the first century AD. Since then, the questions have not ceased. Who or what is the beast? What is the nature of the beast's Mark?[4] What does "666" mean? How do you "calculate the number of his name"? Are these mere symbols, or will the beast be a real man and the Mark a real thing? How close are we to this coming to pass? Before we can dive deeper into these answers, there are a few fundamental terms and biblical concepts we must first define and discuss. This foundation will be critical for the rest of the book.

Can the Impossible Become Inevitable?

Traditionally, those who tried to understand the Mark of the Beast as something tangible, had trouble imagining it. The verses above depict a comprehensive global economic system — too comprehensive for earlier generations to grasp. Their life experiences did not allow them to envision any circumstances where a literal interpretation could be possible.

Still, they had strong evidence of the Bible's veracity — enough to convince them that they could trust it even in those places where they didn't fully understand it. So, they worked hard to imagine scenarios in which this seemingly impossible prophecy had already come true in the past or could come true in the future.

Because they could not fathom a literal interpretation, many decided the Mark must be an allegory. Some imagined it as an ideology or religion. In recent decades, some saw it as a computer system. Others thought it might stand for chronic elements of the human condition such as war, subjugation, or violence.

Those who saw the Book of Revelation as having already

---

[4] When referring to the Mark of the Beast, the phrase "Mark of the Beast" and the word "Mark" will be capitalized in this book for clarity, except in quotations.

happened were used to stretching things in a big way. Many of them decided that coins carrying the image of the Roman emperor must represent the Mark. After all, you can't buy or sell without a coin and sometimes people carry coins in their hands, but you would be hard pressed to find people who carry coins "on their foreheads."

In this book, we will attempt to answer questions regarding the Mark of the Beast using a common rule of conservative Bible scholars. You may have heard it before. It's true for Bible interpretation in general, but it is especially helpful in understanding prophecy...

When the literal sense makes good sense, seek no other sense lest it result in nonsense.

As we will see, when it comes to the Bible's claims regarding the Mark of the Beast, new technology makes a literal fulfillment not only possible, but inevitable.

Who is the Beast?

According to Revelation 13:18, "the number of the beast" is "the number of a man." That tells us something crucial. The beast is not just a symbol, but a flesh and blood human male. The Bible depicts him as a head of government who becomes the totalitarian leader of the world. He will promise utopia, but his actions will trigger a time of unprecedented disaster.

Daniel 8:23-24 says, "When the transgressors have reached their fullness, A king shall arise, Having fierce features, Who understands sinister schemes. His power shall be mighty, but not by his own power; He shall destroy fearfully, And shall prosper and thrive."

At first, it may sound self-contradictory to say, "His power shall be mighty, but not by his own power." But Revelation 13:2 explains exactly what that means. "The dragon gave him his power, his throne, and great authority."

Who is the Dragon?

Revelation 12:9 identifies "the dragon" as Satan himself. "So the great dragon was cast out, that serpent of old, called the Devil and Satan, who deceives the whole world." We see the same identification in Revelation 20:2. "The dragon, that serpent of old, who is the Devil and Satan."

It could not be clearer. Some people say, "the Devil" and some people say, "Satan." Both words describe the same being. Finally, both verses reach back to the dawn of humanity and the Garden of Eden, identifying this entity as "that serpent of old." This leaves no doubt.

The "dragon" is the devil, and Revelation 13:2 says, "The dragon gave him his power." That is why Daniel says the Antichrist's "power shall be mighty, but not by his own power." The dragon — "that serpent of old" — will directly empower the beast.

Who is the Second Beast?

Revelation 13:11 says, "Then I saw another beast coming up out of the earth." The first beast is the Antichrist. The second beast is "the false prophet." The pronoun "he" in Revelation 13:16 refers to the false prophet when it says, "He causes all… to receive a mark on their right hand or on their foreheads."

Revelation 13:12-18 describes the false prophet as both a propagandist for the Antichrist and an enforcer of the Antichrist's rule. He deceives people into worshiping the first beast, and he punishes them if they refuse.

Can the Mark of the Beast Be Understood at Face Value?

The Bible sometimes uses symbols. The Book of Revelation is full of them. But we cannot assign allegory status haphazardly. We must let the Bible itself distinguish between the symbolic and the literal. When we encounter what seems like a symbol, we must look to the Bible — not our own imaginations — for the correct interpretations.

For centuries, Bible expositors struggled to understand how the Mark of the Beast could be literal since the literal implementation seemed impossible at the time. To make it fit with their understanding of the world, they tended to compromise it, spiritualize it, or deny it. But the once "unfathomable" elements of the Bible's description of the Mark in our time have come to seem routine. Even so, much of Christendom holds to these traditions instead of embracing the Bible directly.

The words "Mark of the Beast" describe the thing from God's point of view. Obviously, the Antichrist will not identify himself as "the Antichrist" or "the beast." And he won't call his monetary control system "the Mark of the Beast." But we can take the words literally because they accurately depict the Mark from God's perspective. He sees the Antichrist as a beast and his Mark as the Mark of the Beast.

PART ONE: QUESTIONS AND ANSWERS

CHAPTER 2

Beastly Deceptions

The Antichrist has not yet been revealed to the world. But the person behind Antichrist, Satan,[5] has been hard at work throughout human history.[6] The Antichrist does not have to be present for his program to be in operation.[7] As we come closer to the time of the Antichrist, his program accelerates. We can already see it, especially in the satanic deceptions at work in the world right now.

What is the Mark's Purpose?

The Mark of the Beast will be a government program, and government programs are always presented as solutions to prob-

---

[5] Revelation 13:4

[6] Genesis 3

[7] 1 John 2:18

lems. By examining the nature of the Mark of the Beast, we can discern a great deal about the problems it will purport to solve.

- The Mark will control commerce (buying and selling), making it an economic system. Therefore, it will be implemented with the promise of solving an *economic problem*.

- The Mark will be a global system. Revelation 13:3 says, "All the world... followed the beast." Revelation 13:8 says, "All who dwell on the earth will worship him, whose names have not been written in the Book of Life." So, when Revelation 13:16 says the false prophet "causes all... to receive a mark," the context tells us that he will order all the people of earth to receive it. That means the problem it addresses will be a *global problem*.

- The Mark is an extreme solution. It means that the world's nations will give up a significant portion of their sovereignty. Only the immediate threat of catastrophe or the aftermath of a catastrophe would push them to such an extreme solution. Also, the system will exclude the unmarked from all buying and all selling. And people will submit. That's super extreme! We know, therefore, that it will be presented as a solution to an extreme problem — a fix for a *catastrophe*.

- So, the Mark of the Beast will be meant to solve or avert a *global economic catastrophe*.

PART ONE: QUESTIONS AND ANSWERS

Could Things Really Get That Bad?

From China to the United States, from Saudi Arabia to the European Union, deficit spending now endangers all the world's economies. According to the International Monetary Fund, global debt surged 28% in 2020 alone. At the end of that year, it stood at an astounding 256% of the world's GDP.[8] Those figures are from 2020 when global debt had "only" risen to $226 trillion. In 2021, that number exploded to a record $303 trillion according to the Institute of International Finance.

Unless corrected, these growing levels of debt will lead to hyperinflation[9] [10] [11] and/or a global economic collapse. In November of 2022, MarketWatch ran a story with the headline, "Hedge-fund giant Elliott warns looming hyperinflation could lead to 'global societal collapse.'" The hedge-fund firm sent out a letter to clients saying that the world is "on the path to hyperinflation," and that this could lead to "global societal collapse and civil or international strife."

---

[8] GDP stands for "Gross Domestic Product." GDP is defined as "the total monetary or market value of all the finished goods and services produced within a country's borders in a specific time period." In this case, we're talking about a period of one year. It is a measure of the entire economic output of each nation during that year compared to total debt. The nations are "underwater."

[9] In 2018, Venezuela's inflation rate exceeded 100,000%. That's hyperinflation. It destroys savings, businesses, banks, households, and every other entity that uses money, and it destroys them fast.

[10] Indebted governments like inflation because it lowers the value of the money they owe, making it easier to either pay off or at least stay afloat. But it is self-perpetuating until it eventually implodes.

[11] The Bible describes hyperinflation as a last-days phenomenon in Revelation 6:6 where it warns that a loaf of bread made with wheat will cost a day's wage for the average working person.

They wrote, "Investors should not assume they have 'seen everything.'" They pointed out that the world now faces something far more serious than the 1987 crash, the dot-com bust, or 2008's so-called "great recession."

Hyperinflation, economic collapse, or the threat of them could force the world's governments to accept Antichrist's extreme solutions. Believers know the Mark of the Beast will happen because the Bible says it will. But even from a secular perspective, world leaders are now taking actions that make fulfillment of these prophesies seem inevitable.

How Will They Sell the Mark to the Public?

In addition to economic security, leaders will sell the Mark in terms of safety, prosperity, and convenience. They will even throw in things like social justice, financial equity, and solving climate change. They will present it as a matter of life and death.

As to privacy concerns, we have already seen that people are fully willing to exchange privacy for convenience. The Mark will include both convenience and health. Almost no one frets when Emergency Room workers remove a patient's clothes. With health or even life at stake, privacy takes a backseat.

The Mark will also promise increased security against crime and a way to stop human activity from causing more global warming.

How Will God View the Mark?

The Mark will purport to do good in hundreds of ways. So, even if some authorities use the Mark in bad ways, we might feel tempted to see it as a mixture of good and evil. But the Bi-

PART ONE: QUESTIONS AND ANSWERS

ble leaves no room for doubt. The Mark will be an abomination to God — pure evil.

Revelation 13:16-18, 14:9-13, 15:2, 16:2, 19:20, and 20:4 all contain references to the Antichrist in association with his Mark. These verses show that in God's eyes, the Mark is hideously vile, a sign of mankind's ultimate choice of evil over good — a final rejection of Him.

Why is this so serious? It is very possible that the Mark, directly or indirectly, could permanently alter human DNA *EUGENICS* causing people to become something other than what we were created to be. In God's eyes, this act, by definition, would make us an abomination. No longer being something that was created in His own image. But even worse, doing such a thing willingly is the ultimate rejection of God's plan because you have replaced Him, with yourself. *TRANSGENDER*

We see how God views the Mark when we look at His reaction to those who receive it. Revelation 14:11 uses a strongly worded, intense warning to those who would receive the Mark. "And the smoke of their torment ascends forever and ever; and they have no rest day or night, who worship the beast and his image, and whoever receives the mark of his name."

Will People Receive the Mark by Trickery, Accident, or Deception?

The verse we just read tells the horrific consequences of receiving the Mark. Such outcomes are no casual thing to God. He will hold recipients of the Mark accountable because they will choose to receive it. Nor will the Mark be a vague decision. It will be a bold line in the sand, and no one will cross that line accidentally.

While it will be a clear and conscious choice made by each individual, great deception will also be involved...

And he [the false prophet] deceives those who dwell on the earth by those signs which he was granted to do in the sight of the beast.
— *Revelation 13:14*

If great deception is involved, how is it still considered one's choice? Worship is a theme in the Book of Revelation. It's mentioned 24 times — mostly in concerning the worship of God. But 11 of the 24 times, it refers to the worship of Satan or the Antichrist. True worship is an act of the will. It is a choice. The prohibition against worshiping anyone or anything other than the true God is a theme running throughout scripture.

Revelation repeatedly connects the Mark of the Beast to the *worship* of the Antichrist and, through him, worship of Satan. Revelation 14:9-10 says, "If anyone worships the beast and his image, and receives his mark on his forehead or on his hand, he himself shall also drink of the wine of the wrath of God." Revelation 16:2 says, "A foul and loathsome sore came upon the men who had the mark of the beast and those who *worshiped* his image." [Emphasis added.]

The Mark will involve both choice and deception. That is not a contradiction. The Bible gives us many instances in which people choose and are simultaneously deceived. But let's be clear. That usually means they chose to be deceived. Being deceived through lack of discernment means that at some point in life, the individual chose to give up the ability to discern truth from lie. In that sense, they willingly rejected future opportunities to see biblical truth.

That's what will happen here. Blasphemy against God will characterize the Antichrist's speech.[12] He will rail against the Christians already in heaven[13] and will make war against their counterparts still on earth.[14] They will hear an angelic warning[15] and know that they are choosing to side with God's enemy. It will not be a trick and it will not be an accident. They will *know*!

Romans 1:25 speaks of the choice to be deceived when it says they "exchanged the truth of God for the lie." 2 Timothy 4:3 says that a time is coming when people will "not endure sound doctrine." The Greek here translated "not endure" literally means they "won't put up with it." Sound doctrine — the thing they won't put up with — is truth. They will choose not to put up with truth. WILLFULLY IGNORANT

Continued willful rejection of truth leads to dreadful things. God gives them over to the lies for which they long. Romans 1:28 says, "Even as they did not like to retain God in their knowledge, God gave them over to a debased mind."

2 Thessalonians 2:9-10 talks about this terrible-yet-just-phenomenon as it relates to the Antichrist (the lawless one). "The coming of the lawless one," it says, "is according to the working of Satan, with all power, signs, and lying wonders, and with all unrighteous deception among those who perish, because they did not receive the love of the truth, that they might be saved."

They will fall for unrighteous deception specifically because they do not want the truth. 1 Timothy 4:1 in the *English*

---

[12] Revelation 13:5-7

[13] Ibid.

[14] Ibid.

[15] Revelation 14:9-11

Standard Version[16] says, "The Spirit expressly says that in later times some will depart from the faith by devoting themselves to deceitful spirits." They will *devote* themselves to spirits of deceit. This illustrates both the choice to be deceived and the spiritual nature of last days deception.

The Antichrist and false prophet will use deception to promulgate the Mark of the Beast, but again, it will be a deception chosen by the deceived.

What Will Happen to the Unmarked?

The law of that day will require every person on the face of the earth to receive the Mark. No one will be exempt, no matter how wealthy or powerful. "He causes all, both small and great, rich and poor, free and slave, to receive a mark...."

Romans 13:1-2 tells us to obey human law. But Acts 5:29 gives a crucial exception. "Peter and the other apostles answered and said: 'We ought to obey God rather than men.'" When human law conflicts with God's law, God's law must take precedence.

When it comes to receiving the Mark of the Beast, some people will choose to obey God rather than man. They will refuse the Mark. Revelation 13:17 says people who refuse it will not be allowed to "buy or sell." Think about what that means.

Think about food. The unmarked will initially have to survive on things they can grow or kill. But most people are not farmers or ranchers. And those who are, can expect strict regulation. Also, farming and animal husbandry require many kinds of purchases. In urban areas, most wildlife will quickly disappear,

---

[16] "ESV" and "English Standard Version" are registered trademarks of Good News Publishers.

leaving unmarked city dwellers and suburbanites to subsist on rats, mice, and bugs. Even in rural areas, wildlife will become scarce.

What could be more alarming, is that the consequences of not being able to buy or sell goes far beyond food. How many people can make their own insulin, or essential drugs? A person may already own a car, but they will not be able to buy fuel for it or pay for licensing and registration. With real estate taxes unpaid, government will take homes away. Fortunes will disappear in a matter of days or even hours.

The unmarked will initially suffer incredible hardship, but this will quickly become persecution and death by order of the second beast and all who follow the Antichrist. Revelation 13:15 says that the beast will cause as many as would not worship his image to be killed.

Does This Mean One-world Government?

Yes. But unknowing to most, the global government prophesied at the end of days won't be the first. So, what was and why does it matter?

MARKING THE MASSES

PART ONE: QUESTIONS AND ANSWERS

CHAPTER 3

Spire of Babel

History is filled with ambitious leaders trying to expand their nations' borders until they encompassed everything and everyone. Of them all, only one succeeded, and only briefly. His name was Nimrod. He was a descendant of Noah's son Ham.

Through Adam and later through Noah, God admonished humanity to, "Be fruitful and multiply, and fill the earth."[17] They were fruitful and multiplied. But after the flood, people seemed to have been reluctant to fill the earth. Perhaps because of fear, they stuck together, eventually migrating to the Plains of Shinar in modern day Iraq.

How Could Nimrod Keep His One-World Government?

---

[17] Genesis 1:28, Genesis 8:15-17

On those plains, Nimrod founded a great city that he named "Babel" and ordered the construction of a tower that would reach into the heavens. It would be the largest manmade object on the face of the Earth.

The tower meant that Nimrod's city could provide safety against the whims of capricious gods or the judgment of Yahweh, the God of Nimrod's Great Grandfather, Noah. In the case of another flood, the tower would save them! Although the world's inhabitants might have seen Nimrod as a type of "savior", with Babel as their safe haven, the true intent for this one world government was an attempt for man to protect himself against the wrath of God and His righteous judgement. Also, this was in clear defiance of God's commandment.

In Genesis 11:4, the leaders say to one another, "Come, let us build ourselves a city, and a tower whose top is in the heavens; let us make a name for ourselves, lest we be scattered abroad over the face of the whole earth." But God commanded them to fill the earth.

Take a step back from this story and the reason for the tower becomes obvious — it was an attempt to maintain a one-world government by convincing inhabitants to not scatter abroad. This could be accomplished because Nimrod was providing what no one else could. Peace and safety. Of course, this would only be an illusion.

For God to enforce His command for humanity to fill the earth, He didn't bring forth another great flood (He promised not to). He simply and mercifully confused their language. Breakdowns in communication stopped the tower's construction, and as a result, the people left Babel, scattered to the four corners of the Earth. Nimrod's plan to establish and maintain a one-world government had failed.

PART ONE: QUESTIONS AND ANSWERS

How Can a Disjointed World Unite Once Again?

Since then, clashing languages and cultures have segregated populations within opposing nations and regions for millennia — compounding a long history of perception that an overarching world ruler could never succeed again — that is, until recently.

For most of human history, a one-world government was the ambition of dictators and tyrants. But about 150 years ago, it also became a cause *célèbre* among the intelligentsia. It gained momentum during the time when men believed technology was about to turn earth into a paradise. World government making utopia possible was a strong argument for some. But after the two World Wars, they found an even more persuasive argument. They said world government was necessary for the survival of civilization. Sound familiar?

As we look at the push for global government over the last century and a half, there are several important things to notice. First, note the role that fear of widespread death and destruction plays. It comes up again and again as a motivating factor.

Second, look at the global elite's fear of the masses, their consequent fear of actual democracy, and the extreme measures they take to gain control of regular people. To see their desperation, look at the extreme solutions they tried, including mass sterilization and mass murder. Notice that the advocates of these things were not people from the fringe of society. They were the mainstream... and they still are.

Their solution? World government. But until recently, it was a practical impossibility. Unlike Nimrod's one world government, many today believe the earth is now too populated and complex for a single government or person to control. For the elites of today to accomplish what Nimrod attempted to do thousands of years ago, drastic changes would have to occur to shrink the world back down to a manageable size.

PART TWO

Follow the Science

MARKING THE MASSES

PART TWO: FOLLOW THE SCIENCE

CHAPTER 4

Technology Shrinks the Earth

Since the Great Flood, new empires have come and gone over millennia. Each had a hub of power, such as Babylon or Rome. Yet most of the real governing took place far from the great capital cities. Provincial governors and the leaders of military garrisons held most of the control over citizens' lives. If the locals paid their taxes, they usually heard little from the governor and less from the emperor. The earth was too big for government to be what the Bible describes for the last days — both global and local.

As the centuries passed, better roads and boat designs slightly shortened travel times. But the real change began in 1844 when Samuel Morse initiated his electric telegraph system. That year, over a wire stretching from Washington to Baltimore, Morse transmitted four words from the Bible. "What hath God wrought!"[18] With that transmission, the world was transformed. It shrank. The planet's physical dimensions did not change, but new technology brought the earth's people closer together.

When the first useful transatlantic telegraph went into operation, advertisers used the slogan, "Two weeks to two minutes." No one had yet coined the term "snail mail," but that is what postal mail had already become. In two minutes, an American could now reach across the ocean and touch Europe.

Harnessing electricity had been the key. In the decades since then, use of electricity has given us an ever-growing stream of seemingly magical abilities. Soon, telephones made the earth smaller still. With the phone, human beings could, in the comfort of their homes, reach out across the world. And it was personal — not dots and dashes, but human voices spoken in one place and replicated in another.

The World in Your Living Room

Telephones sent ordinary voices to the whole earth. Phonographs brought extraordinary voices from concert stages around their world into the living rooms of ordinary people. It brought different cultures close to one another, sometimes closer than the people next door.

Broadcast radio did many of those same things. Joe the Kansas farmer finished his day's work, went inside his home, ate his supper, then walked into the living room and turned on the radio. It transmitted ideas he had not previously considered. It brought him news of the world. With that news came theatrical and musical performances from the world's great venues.

---

[18] Numbers 23:23

PART TWO: FOLLOW THE SCIENCE

He became — without meaning to or even knowing it — cosmopolitan. Technology did not just make the world smaller; it made Joe larger.

Cameras and film became inexpensive enough for regular people, and the images would often outlast the people in them and those who took them.

Inventors then strung photographs together to create motion pictures. Suddenly, tall tales of ancient campfire lore came to life. A trip to the nickelodeon, and later to the theater, meant transcending time and place. People watched moving images of history's most glorious achievements, mankind's highest adventures, and some of its most tawdry. The prettiest, funniest, most dramatic people in the world entered the room and stood closer than a dear friend.

Stories congealed on celluloid carried viewers into the worlds of the rich, famous, and powerful. It took audiences back into history or forward into fantasies of the future. It gave them heroes and heroines with whom to identify, and with whom they could vicariously share triumph or love. It made hidden reality visible, and allowed them to see the impossible with their own eyes. Filmed images engulfed viewers in worlds known and unknown — in horrors, delights, humor, sensuality, and adventure.

Then — maybe the next minute, the next hour, or next week — the viewer could experience it again in exactly the same way.

Such inventions had the practical effect of making the entire planet smaller than the Plains of Shinar in the days of Babel. It took far less time to make an intercontinental phone call than to send a message from one side of that ancient plain to the other.

Technology and the Promise of Peace

In the early days of the 20th century, some believed that technology would soon produce the most dramatic change in human history — an end to war. They saw the two main causes of war as a lack of communication and the scarcity of goods. Technology addressed both.

Utopian dreamers reasoned that communication enables understanding and understanding reduces the urge for conflict. Therefore, instead of fighting out their differences, they believed nations of the future would use technology to talk out their differences. Build a red telephone. Send a wire. Negotiate. Talk and listen. Technology would make it easy.

Technology also addressed the issue of scarcity. By the beginning of the 20th century, technical innovations had already allowed humanity to produce an abundance of goods never dreamed of by previous generations. In 1902, H. G. Wells said, "The development of science has lifted famine and pestilence from the shoulders of man, and it will yet lift war."[19]

Industrialized Death

The arrival of World War I hammered hard against these views. Instead of applying the new technologies to peace, the war appropriated them for itself. It industrialized killing and destruction, creating a horror show like the world had never seen.

World War II was worse. Even before the atomic bombs,

---

[19] *Anticipations: Of the Reaction of Mechanical and Scientific Progress upon Human life and Thought* by Herbert George Wells, Chapman & Hall, Ld., 1902.

PART TWO: FOLLOW THE SCIENCE

Tokyo, Berlin, and other large population centers experienced unprecedented and horrific bombings. When world leaders like Harry Truman saw the damage instigated by their own orders, they were aghast. Truman, a veteran of World War I, wrote in his diary, "I never saw such destruction." He called it an "absolute ruin." He went on, "I fear that machines are ahead of morals by some centuries and when morals catch up there'll be no reason for any of it."

Truman said to others, "It is a terrible thing, but they brought it on themselves." Winston Churchill seemed to see it as a warning. "This is what would have happened to us if they had won the war. We would have been in the bunker."

After the Second World War, the surviving Wright brother, Orville spoke of his sadness that he and his brother's invention had been the instrument of so much pain and destruction. He said, "We dared to hope we had invented something that would bring lasting peace to the earth. But we were wrong."

Orville said that he did not regret his role in the airplane's invention, "though no one could deplore more than I do the destruction it has caused." He explained, "I feel about the airplane much the same as I do in regard to fire. That is, I regret all the terrible damage caused by fire, but I think it is good for the human race that someone discovered how to start fires and that we have learned how to put fire to thousands of important uses."

Tools amplify the good and the bad of their users. Humans use airplanes, hammers, engines, and plows to do the things humans want done. And people fight. They fight for good reasons and bad. But they fight. To change this would require a basic change in humanity.

The two world wars, along with the failure of peace efforts that preceded them, convinced elites of four things. 1—Continued technical innovation would mean the destruction of humanity unless people stopped fighting wars. 2—They must bring human impulses under control, meaning that they must bring human beings under control. 3—Science must be given a free hand in human affairs. 4—To be effective, the changes must be universal. Therefore, the continued existence of human civilization required world government.

To one extent or another, elites still hold to these ideas. One day such thinking will lead to a global totalitarian government and the Mark of the Beast.

Shrinking the world through technology may once again allow the rise of a one world government, but this alone isn't sustainable. As in the days of Nimrod, true global control cannot be entirely forced as was attempted by countless dictators and tyrants throughout the ages, but rather also needs to be desired by the people themselves. In order to win the hearts of the people, science, rather than mere technology, becomes the weapon.

PART TWO: FOLLOW THE SCIENCE

CHAPTER 5

Science: The World's New Master

What we call "science" comes in two distinct flavors. One is science as defined by the Science Council — "the pursuit and application of knowledge and understanding of the natural and social world following a systematic methodology based on evidence."[20] Science by that definition requires humility.

When I speak of science as the world's new master, I'm not talking about science "following a systematic methodology based on evidence." I'm talking about a popularized and politicized thing that carries the label "science." Sometimes it speaks the truth and sometimes it theorizes the ridiculous.

Popularized science means science dumbed down to a point where a short article can seem to explain something as intricate

---

[20] The Science Council is a UK institution established by Royal Charter in 2003.

and complex as the human brain. *Politicized* science is a means to political ends. It says what its political masters tell it to say. Both popularized science and politicized science reinforce common prejudices and serve the thought-fashions of the moment. Together, they become the means to an end — preserving power for the elite. *COVID VIRUS - CASE IN POINT*

Science popularizers have existed since a long-ago father explained to his son that a tree grows because a spirit lives inside. Popularizers have always had a knack for presenting "science" in ways that make sense to the layman. They give the ordinary person an impression that he knows all the pertinent facts about a topic upon which he may now know less than when the explanation began.

Greta Thunberg

In 2018 at the age of 15, Greta Thunberg became an international celebrity for protesting outside the Swedish parliament. With good PR, she became a media sensation. Forbes soon recognized her as one of the "most influential people in the world." A year later, she had become Time Magazine's "Person of the Year."

The United Nations invited her to the General Assembly Hall to address their Climate Action Summit. When she spoke, she berated them as hypocrites, failures, and thieves. They listened with grave, understanding faces.

With extreme histrionics, her face contorting with self-pity and bestial rage, she said, "You have stolen my dreams and my childhood with your empty words. And yet I'm one of the lucky ones. People are suffering. People are dying. Entire ecosystems are collapsing. We are in the beginning of a mass extinction, and all you can talk about is money and fairy tales of eternal economic growth. How dare you!"

When launching a new book, let the world know that her concerns do not end with "climate change." This is good because the climate has been changing since God created the earth. She also wants to overthrow "the whole capitalist system." She called capitalism the source of "colonialism, imperialism, oppression, genocide." The truth is just the opposite. When it works properly, capitalism provides opportunity. For the poor, it creates avenues of ascent. It empowers the underprivileged, protects the vulnerable, and gives all who live under it hope for a better life and a better world. Compare its track record with any other economic system, and it wins hands down.

I don't blame Greta. She probably really believes that the men and women of the United Nations stole her childhood. Instead of crediting capitalism for the boon it has been to her life, she seems to really blame them for somehow oppressing her. She has been diagnosed with Asperger syndrome, obsessive–compulsive disorder (OCD), and selective mutism, none of which diminishes her intelligence. But they do make her the kind of speaker who can stir up a camp meeting — or an anti-global warming gathering.

Radical environmentalists, socialists, and globalists have used her unique talents for their own purposes. The more extreme her words and behavior, the more applause she receives. Her special brand of rage leads many of the young to despair, but it helps her sponsors raise money.

Greta clearly doesn't understand the science behind her statements, but it's the perfect avenue to convince the world that it needs to seek a new age of peace and safety.

Climate Mania

In his speech at the 27th annual UN Climate Conference (COP27), President Biden promised the United States will "do our part to avert" a "climate hell." He added, "We're not ignoring harbingers that are already here. So many disasters — the climate crisis is hitting hardest those countries and communities that have the fewest resources to respond."

We live in political climate where politicians and the media blame every hurricane, every tornado, every drought, and every flood on climate change. Even in years when there are fewer tornadoes and hurricanes than normal, when they happen the blame goes to climate change. All this creates a mounting fear for the future.

Media mogul Ted Turner has said that by 2040 and no later than 2050, the only humans left on earth will be cannibals. In 2008, he told Charlie Rose on PBS, "We'll be eight degrees hotter in 30 or 40 years and basically none of the crops will grow…. Most of the people will have died and the rest of us will be cannibals. Civilization will have broken down. The few people left will be living in a failed state — like Somalia or Sudan — and living conditions will be intolerable."

Most of those who believe such dire predictions are under the age of twenty-five. Among those in that age range, many have given up on life. They've taken an "eat, drink, and be merry"[21] attitude. Enjoy it while you live. It puts a dark tinge on anything approaching joy. Corporations and the media crave the approval of the young. They play to their fears even as they sell the very products that generate the pollution that is claimed to

---

[21] Luke 12:19

be destroying the world.

Those global-warming true believers who still hope to reverse climate change see the unalarmed as the problem.

Herbert George Wells and a New World Order

Today, when we think of science popularizers, we might think of Neil deGrasse Tyson. A generation ago, it would have been Carl Sagan. But history's most influential science popularizer was a man named H. G. Wells. It's hard now to grasp Wells' impact on the world. Today, if we think of him at all, it is usually in connection with a few of his early science fiction novels. *The Time Machine* was his first book, quickly followed by *War of the Worlds*, *The Invisible Man*, and *The Island of Doctor Moreau* — all published from 1895 to 1897.

That was only the beginning. Between 1895 and his death in 1946, he wrote more than one hundred books on a variety of topics. He also wrote thousands of articles and gave thousands of lectures. Wells' success with science fiction gave both him and the public a belief that he understood humanity's past and future. He and his readers saw him as a guide through times of turmoil and change. They and he believed he understood the promise and peril of new and coming technologies. He wrote fiction about utopian worlds. He wrote even more about how to create utopia on earth. Most of that turned out to be fiction as well.

People paid attention. Most of his books were best sellers. He was nominated for the Nobel Prize in Literature in 1921, 1932, 1935, and 1946. Winston Churchill read his works and borrowed memorable phrases from them. A principal author of the United Nation's Universal Declaration of Human Rights, called Wells' tract, "The Rights of Man," one of their leading influences.

The writer of 1984, George Orwell, often criticized Wells. But he also gave H. G. his due. Orwell wrote, "Thinking people who were born about the beginning of this century are in some sense Wells' own creation. How much influence any mere writer has, and especially a 'popular' writer whose work takes effect quickly, is questionable, but I doubt whether anyone who was writing books between 1900 and 1920, at any rate in the English language, influenced the young so much. The minds of all of us, and therefore the physical world, would be perceptibly different if Wells had never existed."

Science in Charge

Wells was a free-love, one-world government socialist. He saw global governance as the only path to peace. He was among the first to recognize the destructive potential of future war technologies. He correctly forecast that such technologies would eventually threaten human survival.

Yet to Wells, one-world government was not enough. It would not succeed if it were merely a bigger version of what already existed. That left too much to chance. He believed that the only successful government would be one that always and invariably follows the science. Science would be the world's new master. For him, that meant putting technocrats in charge of everything.

Wells believed that smart, emotionally uninvolved, scientists could solve all mankind's problems if given the means and authority to do so. He saw them much like he imagined the Martians in *War of the Worlds*, with "intellects vast and cool and unsympathetic."

They would rule according to mathematical calculations — not emotions. They would base their decisions on the greater good of the human enterprise as a whole — not on the sentimental value often placed on the individual. Technocrats would run civilization according to hard facts. He predicted a time when productivity, not feelings, would decide a person's worth.

The problem with popular science is that it tends to become religion. When that happens, science ceases to be real science, but it keeps the façade. Once accepted as religion, science can no longer be questioned.[22] That makes the religion of scientism almost unstoppable.

When science becomes religion, it doesn't simply mean it becomes trusted as the truth, but rather that it replaces God as the truth. In order for the world to accept and be ruled by unsympathetic calculation, science must dismantle the belief that our morals, emotions and even creation itself was designed and intended by a higher power.

---

[22] I realize that I could be criticized here because I am a Christian minister, and Christianity is considered a religion. But I'm not condemning the idea of religion. I'm condemning the idea of science as religion. My claims are based on God's revelation as shown in the Bible. It is faith, but it is not blind faith. It is reasonable. The evidence for it is so strong that it has become the basis of my entire belief system. But even then, I ask questions. My fellow Christians and I often disagree regarding interpretations of the Bible. However, because we trust the Bible as true, we go back to that base by which we measure our beliefs. Science doesn't claim to have heard directly from God. Therefore, everything must be questioned. I am not condemning that. I think it's great. It has been a boon to the world. But it should never be regarded as divinely revealed and therefore beyond questioning. When it is so regarded, it becomes dangerous.

PART TWO: FOLLOW THE SCIENCE

CHAPTER 6

Making Man in Our Own Image

Charles Darwin permeated the thinking of H. G. Wells and a science-based one world government like water permeates tea. And so it was with the rest of the intelligentsia of that age. Even more than today, they saw everything according to a Darwinian model. Darwin published *On the Origin of Species by Means of Natural Selection, or the Preservation of Favoured Races in the Struggle for Life* in 1859. In less than 20 years, the scientific community came to fully embraced the idea of evolution by means of natural selection.

Darwinian phrases like, "survival of the fittest" and "struggle for existence," transcended their biological origins. Elites used Darwin to justify a multitude of ancient prejudices, mostly centered on racism. Elites believed they and their ancestors had risen in society because they were "the fittest." Many believed, for instance, that the African continent was impoverished and should be governed by Europeans because white Europeans were the "favored race" — favored by evolution.

But there was a problem. The forces of Darwinian science and that of technology were on a collision course.

Men Like Gods

In *The Time Machine*, Wells' time traveler goes to the far distant year of 802,701 AD. He finds that over the course of 800 millennia, humans devolved into two distinct species — the grotesque Morlocks and the weak, lazy, apathetic, stupid, and hedonistic Eloi. Morlocks evolved from the working class and Eloi from the elite. Neither one turned out too well. That was Wells' fear — that the evolutionary course of humanity would turn downward — that it would degenerate and devolve.

Wells shifted between great optimism and dark despair. In *Men Like Gods*, he felt optimistic. It ended with a vision for great and positive upheaval on earth. He wrote, "All the conflicts and insurrections and revolutions that had ever been on Earth were but indistinct preludes of the revolution that has still to come."

His protagonist changes into a revolutionary. "It was borne in upon Mr. Barnstaple that he belonged now soul and body to the Revolution, to the Great Revolution that is afoot on Earth; that marches and will never desist nor rest again until old Earth is one city and Utopia set up therein."

At his most optimistic, Wells imagined a future where humans evolved into ever godlike beings. At his most pessimistic, he imagined technology creating an ease of life that would eventually turn people into Elois. To become like gods, humans needed evolution to be working full bore — eliminating slackers and miscreants, "selecting" the best among us for survival and success.

But technology seemed to be working against evolution.

Technology Derails Evolution

Technology's promise of peace was based on a world without want. If all nations and all people had plenty, they would have nothing left to fight over. But plenty for all would also end competition. It would render meaningless such evolutionary creeds as "natural selection" and "survival of the fittest." Abundance selects everyone. Plenty means the survival even of the least fit.

This meant that stupid, lazy, and ill-formed individuals would not only survive, but reproduce. The ill-begotten would "contaminate" human bloodlines, perhaps to the point of extinction. Human technologies were about to end the fight for survival that evolutionists believed necessary for the continued success of the species. They thought a world of plenty meant the end of human evolution and the beginning of human devolution.

Two futures beckoned — utopia or destruction, heaven on earth or hell all over the place.

Their answer was to find a way to take the primal power of evolution into their own hands. Humans had a long history of grabbing hold of nature's power and using it for their good. Surely, they could do that with evolution — take it into their own hands and force it to become profitable to the human enterprise. But how?

Directed Evolution

The great thinkers thought and the great ponderers pondered. How could humans control something so huge as evolution? Humanity tamed other forces of nature, then put them to use. Could they do that with evolution?

Different thinkers at different places in the world all came to the same conclusion at almost the same time. It fell like ripe fruit from Darwin's tree. Humankind, they realized, had already been directing the "evolution" of crops and livestock for hundreds or even thousands of years. Humans had long ago harnessed the power of genetics through selective breeding. For humans to evolve into ever higher forms of existence during an age of plenty, they must find ways to apply this process of selective breeding to the human animal.

And thus, was born one of history's great evils — eugenics.

PART TWO: FOLLOW THE SCIENCE

CHAPTER 7
People of the Abyss

Merriam-Webster.com defines "eugenics" as, "the practice or advocacy of controlled selective breeding of human populations (as by sterilization) to improve the population's genetic composition."[23]

From the late 18th century until the end of World War II, eugenics was the popular "science" of the hour. Eugenicists wanted people of good breeding to do more breeding. But to whatever extent possible, they must stop the ragtag rabble from procreation. This included people of the wrong color, those who held "regressive" beliefs, the mentally and physically impaired, addicts of various kinds, etc.

In 1896, H. G. Wells wrote an article called, "Human Evolution, an Artificial Process." He saw that mankind was no lon-

---

[23] "Eugenics." *Merriam-Webster.com* Dictionary, Merriam-Webster, www.merriam-webster.com/dictionary/eugenics. Accessed November 7, 2022.

ger subject to "natural selection." So, like his Doctor Moreau, he felt it was time for humanity to take evolution into its own hands.

He knew that people would not allow themselves to be bred like cattle.[24] So, he (and most of the intelligentsia of the time) suggested another way. In 1904, Wells wrote, "It is in the sterilization of failure, and not in the selection of successes for breeding, that the possibility of an improvement of the human stock lies."

Sterilization of Failure

In an appendix to his novel, *State of Fear*, author and filmmaker, Michael Crichton, wrote, "Imagine that there is a new scientific theory that warns of an impending crisis, and points to a way out. This theory quickly draws support from leading scientists, politicians, and celebrities around the world. Research is funded by distinguished philanthropies, and carried out at prestigious universities. The crisis is reported frequently in the media. The science is taught in college and high school classrooms."[25]

Today's society may find it hard to believe that anything with the word science affixed to it could be vile, unjust, and

---

[24] Some German youth groups were an exception. Germany not only sterilized the "unfit," but promoted selective breeding through such projects as the Lebensborn Program. Defiance of their parents' Christian morality was encouraged in the League of German Girls, also known as the League of German Maidens. Pregnancies were encouraged and became so common that the girls began to be derogatorily called, "The League of German Mattresses."

[25] *State of Fear* by Michael Crichton, HarperCollins, 2004.

murderous. But this was all three. Eugenics proves that evil can, and too often does, masquerade as science.

The eugenics movement attracted liberals and conservatives. Twenty-nine states passed sterilization laws. They were just "following the science." The Carnegie and Rockefeller Foundations funded eugenics research. The Rockefeller Foundation continued funding Nazi-led eugenics research in Germany until a few months before the beginning of World War II.

Eugenics Goes Mainstream

Harvard, Yale, Princeton, Stanford, and Johns Hopkins all did eugenics research. The National Academy of Sciences, the American Medical Association, and the National Research Council promoted eugenics as good science. It was, for all practical purposes, a "scientific consensus."

Supporters included Theodore Roosevelt, Woodrow Wilson, Oliver Wendel Holmes, Louis Brandies, Alexander Graham Bell, Margaret Sanger, Leland Stanford, George Bernard Shaw, and many more of the most famous and influential people of the day. A hundred years ago, the most brilliant luminaries and the elite of elites almost all supported eugenics. So how could it possibly be wrong?

Surprisingly few people objected to these deadly and discriminatory ideas. They shouted down those who did object as science-deniers. Margaret Sanger, founder of Planned Parenthood, said, "Fostering the good-for-nothing at the expense of the good is an extreme cruelty... there is no greater curse to posterity than that of bequeathing them an increasing population of imbeciles."

Theodore Roosevelt said, "Society has no business to permit degenerates to reproduce their kind."

The famous botanist, Luther Burbank, said, "Stop permitting criminals and weaklings to reproduce."

Kill, Kill, Kill, Kill, Kill

George Bernard Shaw said, "If we desire a certain type of civilization and culture, we must exterminate the sort of people who do not fit into it." In an article for *The Atlantic*, he wrote, "…the ungovernables, the ferocious, the conscienceless, the idiots, the self-centered myops and morons, what of them? Do not punish them. Kill, kill, kill, kill, kill them."[26]

Shaw's statement raises many questions. When he said "idiot," did he mean the literal definition of idiot from that time? That would be a person with an IQ between zero and 25. Or, did he mean what we usually mean by the word, "someone who acts stupidly"? When he spoke of "morons," did he mean people with an IQ of 51 to 70? Or, are those people okay as long as they aren't self-centered?

The word "myops" means the same thing as "myope." That can be a near-sighted person or someone who lacks a long-range perspective. He surely didn't want to kill all near-sighted people. He must have meant that we should kill "self-centered" people who lack the proper long-range perspective.

The problem is obvious. One person's long-range perspective is another person's foolhardiness. And we all lack long-range perspective sometimes, just as we are all sometimes self-centered. "Ferocious" can mean a person who tends toward

---

[26] "Capital Punishment" by George Bernard Shaw, The Atlantic, June 1948.

violence, or it can mean a person with passionate feelings about a cause. "Ungovernable" might be someone who habitually jaywalks.

His list is subjective. Who would decide which of these people society should kill?

Shaw has been called the leading dramatist of his time. *The Oxford Encyclopedia of Theatre* called Shaw, "arguably the most important English-language playwright after Shakespeare."[27] His many popular plays include *Pygmalion* which became the basis for the musical, My Fair Lady. He won the 1925 Nobel Prize in Literature. Yet by Biblical standards, he was a man with a "reprobate mind."[28]

When the layperson comes into agreement with ideas espoused by acclaimed scientists and celebrated authors, it draws him into a circle of genius by proxy. He thinks what elite thinkers think. He can congratulate himself for being among the clever people. When his favorite celebrity advocates an idea he can agree with, it brings him close to the cool people. When politicians act on those beliefs, it places him at the center of a cause.

Eugenics had the added benefit of giving scientific and social justification to racial and social prejudices. Eugenics allowed people to see themselves as concerned citizens, rather than hate-filled bigots.

---

[27] *The Oxford Encyclopedia of Theatre and Performance*, edited by Dennis Kennedy, Oxford University Press, 2003.

[28] Romans 1:28

Ill-shaped and Ailing

H. G. Wells called his 1901 book, *Anticipations*,[29] "the keystone to the main arch of my work." In it, he referred to the part of humanity that needed sterilization as, "People of the Abyss... frequently spoken of as the Urban Poor." At one point in *Anticipations*, he called them, "the wretched multitudes of the Abyss."

Wells spoke of "a mean-spirited, under-sized, diseased little man, quite incapable of earning a decent living even for himself, married to some underfed, ignorant, ill-shaped, plain and diseased little woman, and guilty of the lives of ten or twelve ugly ailing children." His idea was to "let the Abyss... become a 'hotbed' of sterile immorality." If sexual promiscuity among the sterilized masses is evil, he said, at least "it will be a terminating evil."[30]

In other words, they will die off, we will be rid of them, and science will at least be free to build a better man and a better world.

Germany Followed the Science

To see Social Darwinism in action, we need look no further than Nazi Germany. I know that people love to use the Nazis to prove their points on all kinds of social issues. Nevertheless, Nazis really did believe in eugenics, Social Darwinism, and in "favored races."

---

[29] *Anticipations: Of the Reaction of Mechanical and Scientific Progress upon Human Life and Thought* by Herbert George Wells, Chapman & Hall, Ld., 1902.

[30] As an advocate of "free love," it's unlikely he felt much concern over such things.

For instance, the Nazis invented an x-ray machine that could be hidden behind a counter. It sterilized people without them ever knowing it. They did not put this into general use because forced sterilization proved to be a more efficient and thorough method.

Earlier in this book, I quoted George Orwell praising H. G. Wells, but Orwell was also a fierce critic. In the same article, Orwell showed that the Nazis (who Wells hated) had simply put into practice Wells' own formula for utopia.

"Modern Germany is far more scientific than England," Orwell wrote, "and far more barbarous. Much of what Wells has imagined and worked for is physically there in Nazi Germany. The order, the planning, the State encouragement of science, the steel, the concrete, the aero planes, are all there, but all in the service of ideas appropriate to the Stone Age."[31]

Orwell wrote those words in 1941 before anyone yet knew the extent to which the Nazi machine would enact the policies of eugenics. The results of those polices still shock the world.

Fixing the Abyssians

What a surprise! People didn't want to be bred or sterilized. The real-world application of eugenics did not work.

The Nazis tried it on a huge scale, mostly targeting Jews, but also other "undesirables." When people got a good look at what Nazis had done, they were horrified. Most Germans were also horrified. They wondered how one group of humans could

---

[31] "Wells, Hitler and the World State" by George Orwell, originally published in *Horizon Magazine*, August 1941, here quoted from *All Art is Propaganda: Critical Essays* by George Orwell, Mariner Books, 2008.

do such evil to others.

Hitler succeeded in giving eugenics the bad name it deserved. He did that by putting eugenics into actual practice. Today, much of the world would list him as the most evil man who ever lived. Remember that the "science" of eugenics provided the intellectual foundation for his evil actions.

The belief in eugenics did not die entirely, and some continued to practice it on a small scale. Some are still trying to make it work. But in the popular mind, its day has come and gone.

This left the self-appointed elite world-planners with a dilemma. Surely there was more than one way to fix the Abyssians. What should they do with them? They couldn't allow them to gain any degree of wealth because they would draw too heavily on planetary resources.

Yet the answer had been with them for thousands of years. It was simple. Use them!

Automation was slower in coming than they had expected. Elites realized that they still needed laborers and soldiers. Many caught in the Abyss were rightly angry at unfair practices. World-planners rediscovered old ways to harness that anger. And because the anger could be so useful, they created a cottage industry of ways to keep the anger simmering hot. World-planners used rightly felt frustrations of the poor to gain and hold political power for themselves.

After World War II, a revival of biblically inspired notions of right and wrong,[32] along with a new emphasis on the Consti-

---

[32] Such notions include well-known teachings such as, "You shall not murder" (Exodus 20:13), and, "Whatever you want men to do to you, do also to them" (Matthew 7:12). The Bible teaches in Acts 17:26, "He [God] has made from one blood every nation of men to dwell on all the face of the earth."

tution, changed American thinking, and it spread. Add to that the threat of mass uprisings, and Bernard Shaw's "kill, kill, kill, kill, kill" and Wells' sterilization of the unfit, became nonstarters.

World-planners took a new approach. They found ways to control people of the Abyss. Through education and media, they put handles on them, places to grab. That way they could move them when and where needed. After use, they could easily put them away in storage until needed again.

Wealth, Poverty, and Control

The Abyssians were distasteful to them, but extremely useful. Not only would they turn them into willing servants, but they would also grow the Abyss by drawing in the middle class. They would convert them, educate them, and find ways to watch their every move. Eventually, their new Abyss would encompass just about everyone.

Their new sense of control diminished their old fear of democracy. With language, education, and media, they could not only control communication into and out of the Abyss, they could also shape people's thoughts. Popular uprisings were still possible, but the planners felt confident they could turn such turmoil to their own purposes.

The controls evolved. They became more sophisticated, stronger, and tighter. With the media and education establishments, they redefined words. The words' new meanings superimposed themselves on old thought patterns, changing them.

In 2014, China implemented the first national test of their "social credit score." Western elites applied the concept to businesses with their ESG's (environmental, social, and governance ranking system). Expect them to soon apply similar systems to individuals, and for the systems to become more manipulative and more draconian as time passes.

The Mark of the Beast system will feature the highest degree of government control ever achieved over humanity. That march began where eugenics ended.

PART TWO: FOLLOW THE SCIENCE

CHAPTER 8

"Intellects Vast and Cool and Unsympathetic"

"We are America. We never give up. We never give in. We give back, and we follow the science." Those were the words of President Joe Biden to the National Institutes of Health on February 11, 2021. To the staff at the Centers for Disease Control, he said it again. "Follow the science." As he celebrated 50 million Americans taking the vaccine, the president said, "This administration will follow the science."

The marvels of science surround us. It has done so many amazing things that many wonder why it can't also fix society. At the beginning of the 20th century, the most influential people believed it could. Today the number of believers in a science-led utopia has diminished. But from their perch at the top of the societal pyramid, many elites still believe that, if given a free hand, science can fix just about anything.

Technocrats In Control

Many of today's elites are from Silicon Valley. As a group, they are actively working to create everything from flying cars to humanoid machines into which they believe they will be able to upload their minds before death. They think this will give them eternal life. We often see their tirades against anyone who questions "the science," be it genetically modified foods or mRNA vaccines.

They see what they perceive as ignorance standing in the way of science. They are especially concerned when the "unindoctrinated" or "malinformed" vote. They see the masses as needing shepherds to decide what information they can hear and what should be withhold.

Elites see themselves as the shepherds. Again, we see reflections of H. G. Wells. He wanted those who know the most about a given subject to control that area of society. It works great for elites because they have among their caste, experts on everything.

Adam Kirsch, writing for *The New Yorker* in October of 2011 said, "In book after book, novels and nonfiction alike, Wells hammered home the message that humanity could improve its lot only by entrusting power to a self-selected caste of enlightened technicians, who would rule according to the dictates of science."[33]

Isn't that what "follow the science" means? Following the science means putting specialists in charge of their specialty. Medical people would run medicine. Climate specialists would

---

[33] "Utopian Pessimist: The works, world view, and women of H. G. Wells" by Adam Kirsch, *The New Yorker*, October 10, 2011.

run... well, a lot of things. For instance, we might expect geologists with their knowledge of fossil fuels to be in charge of energy, but climate is a favored science and fossil fuel disfavored. Therefore, the geologist must take a lower tier on the technocratic totem pole.

Confusing, right? Specialists in charge of their specialty would become a nightmare of conflicting and overlapping claims.

Hollywood Weighs In

The message in countless television shows and movies is that scientists should be allowed free rein. Remove the red tape. Give them the money they need and don't mess with oversight. On an October 2022 episode of the new version of the TV series *Quantum Leap*, a Congresswoman shows up to ask questions. She's from the Committee charged with oversight of the government's Quantum Leap project. She's not a busybody. She's doing her job.[34]

The show's main characters have kept the project's activities secret from their superiors and from Congress. The program depicts the Congresswoman as the antagonist, the bad guy. Yet, as a member of Congress, she represents us — the people. Quantum Leap team members lie to her. When she figures out part of what is going on, they blackmail her into not telling others the truth. They claim it is not blackmail, but it clearly is.

Films and television repeat this message over and over. They

---

[34] "Salvation or Bust" directed by Silas Howard and written by Benjamin Raab & Deric A. Hughes, air date October 17, 2022, *Quantum Leap*, created by Donald P. Bellisario.

show the expert as the good guy and government oversight as a force of evil. Films depict the Constitution itself as evil if it interferes with the protagonist's goal. They tell us that experts know what they're doing, and we must always trust them to do the right thing. Therefore, government funding should not bring with it the red tape of government oversight. Taxpayers' money should be spent as decreed by science, and the taxpayers themselves should have no voice in the matter.

Follow the Money

President Biden is not alone in his push to "follow the science" relentlessly. Most politicians, educators, entertainers, and even theologians now claim to "follow the science."

No one ever says, "Let the people with money rule your life." But to "follow the science" consistently means "let science rule." And science depends on funding. With money, the wealthy control science — its focus, direction, and, to a large degree, its conclusions. They do it through their corporations, their foundations, and, mostly, with their influence over government.

"Senator, it's crucial for the country for the government to subsidize research into the mating habits of field mice." So says the campaign contributor who owns a company wanting to reduce its losses to hungry mice.

Despite the flaws of the scientific establishment, most people see science as pure and untainted. But it is political and, like water headed for low ground, it inevitably follows the money.

Scientists are as human as everyone else. They are subject to the same passions. They want to be liked. They do not want to admit when they are wrong. They are subject to pride, lust

PART TWO: FOLLOW THE SCIENCE

for power, and to an ever-present need for funding. Make no mistake. Money fuels and directs science. The profit motive in science has given us many amazing things. But when it seeks to control us, it becomes dangerous.

Enlightened Governance

Remember the old "food pyramid"? Before 2005, it was at least simple and easy to understand. That year they painted stripes on the pyramid. This helped us get more exercise by getting us to scratch our heads. What does the width at the bottom of the pyramid mean now? What do stripes mean as they get skinnier at that top?

But a close look at the striped pyramid at least shows a healthier diet. The old pyramid had a broad base of grains and cereals — carbs. That's what government scientists told us to eat more than anything else. Carbohydrates — the stuff that, if eaten in large quantities, makes people fat, diabetic, exhausted, and prone to heart disease. I'm sure they had our best interest in mind, but it was not a stellar moment for medical technocrats.

The Man Who Was Science

And then there is the strange case of Dr. Anthony Fauci. He's the man who saw himself as science personified. "If you are trying to get at me as a public health official and a scientist," the doctor said, "you're really attacking, not only Dr. Anthony Fauci, you're attacking science."[35]

---

[35] "Fauci says attacks on him are 'attacks on science'" by Carly Ortiz-Lytle, *Yahoo News*, June 9, 2021.

Is it still science when no one can question or criticize its findings? Or is that the point where science places itself in the realm of religion? If to question Anthony Fauci's decisions is a sacrilege against science, then science has ceased to be science. It has become that other thing — that politicized thing masquerading as science.

The Toronto Sun wrote of Fauci, "He became widely regarded as the top authority on all things COVID-related, and his word was accepted by many in the media and general public as the official scientific truth, while contrary opinions, even from credible experts, were often dismissed as conspiracy theory."[36]

In March of 2020, he said, "There's no reason to be walking around with a mask." Later, he not only insisted that people wear masks, he urged governments and businesses to impose mask mandates on the people he once told not to wear masks. He called that, "the scientific process." Fauci explained, "As you get more information, it's essential that you change your opinion, because you've got to be guided by the science and the current data."

In other words, Fauci could question his own opinion, but for anyone else to question that same opinion equaled an attack on science. We all agree that a scientist should follow the evidence and change his mind accordingly. But scientific-sounding Covid pronouncements were coming out of the mouths of health officials as early as January 2020. China first informed the World Health Organization about Covid-19 in late December of 2019. It takes a while to learn about a new disease.

Yet in a March 2020 interview conducted by Dr. Jonathan

---

[36] "Fauci lies and makes mistakes—just like the rest of us," *The Toronto Sun*, June 30, 2021.

LaPook, Fauci doubled down on the certainty of his guesses. Regarding not wearing masks, LaPook asked, "You're sure of it? Because people are listening really closely to this."

With that question LaPook gave the technocrat a perfect opportunity for the humility required by real science. He could have said, "We only learned about this disease a few weeks ago, so I only have preliminary information. Right now, we believe that you will not be helped by wearing a mask."

Instead, he answered with the arrogance of a man who thinks he is the personification of science. "There's no reason to be walking around with a mask," he confidently repeated. "When you're in the middle of an outbreak, wearing a mask might make people feel a little bit better and it might even block a droplet, but it's not providing the perfect protection that people think that it is. And, often, there are unintended consequences — people keep fiddling with the mask and they keep touching their face."

Mom and Dad: The Masked Strangers

I think government mask mandates did more harm than good during the Covid crisis. Several studies showed negligible differences between populations that mandated masks and those that did not.[37] City Journal published a two-line graph. One line showed the weekly rate of Covid cases in all states with mask mandates. The other showed the same thing in states without mask mandates. The two lines track almost perfectly together.

City Journal wrote, "If you add up all the numbers on those

---

[37] "Mask Mandates Didn't Make Much of a Difference Anyway" by Faye Flam, *Bloomberg*, February 11, 2022.

two lines, you find that the mask mandates made zero difference."[38]

If mask mandates did not "control the spread" as officials said they would, then the mandates were a net negative. They didn't help, but they did harm. For instance, they harmed infants in the first crucial months of life when babies have a powerful need to see and emulate their parents' faces. But there was a mask in-between.

I'm pointing out that scientists too often act like voodoo priests, ready with answers before they have good data on which to base those answers. The scientific process means you get to change your mind. But it also requires some level of humility. When science doesn't know the answer, it should say so.

---

[38] "Maskaholics" by John Tierney, *City Journal*, April 18, 2022

PART TWO: FOLLOW THE SCIENCE

CHAPTER 9

Middleman for the Medicine Men

Today, "follow the science" usually means "follow the popular conception of scientific conclusions even on the issues that actual scientists have as yet come to no conclusion." It means, "follow the establishment" because the establishment owns this kind of science.

Real scientists dare not speak too boldly against politicized science. If they do, they instantly lose standing, credibility, and funding. To keep their jobs, prestige, stature, titles and money, scientists must largely follow the party line.

Turning Science into Doctrine

Everyone admires Galileo Galilei, but no one wants to live a 21st century version of his life. We celebrate Galileo for standing up to the Catholic Church of his day — declaring that the Earth was not the center of the Universe. A statement that was considered heresy through misunderstood interpretation of scripture. But Galileo's discoveries did not actually stand against biblical doctrine. The Church took the science of an earlier generation and turned it into dogma. Doctrine not rooted in the Bible eventually crumbles. Galileo was not fighting biblical Christianity. He was fighting what we see as primitive science. By the way, in another 400 years, people will see our science as primitive.[39]

I said earlier than scientists act like voodoo priests, ready with answers even before they know what they're talking about. That may happen because the public treats them like ancient shamans, expecting instant answers to complex questions. No matter whose fault it is, from the beginning of Covid-19, technocrats in government pretended to know all about it even when the disease was new and mostly unstudied.

Fauci and company started making pronouncements on Covid before giving real scientists the time needed to study the disease. They made authoritative pronouncements, then the vast machinery of government backed them up. It was a heady trip for men and women usually confined to labs, drab offices, and peer reviewed articles in specialized journals.

Just before his inauguration in January of 2021, an article in *Science* stated, "Biden said it 'may take many months to get to where we need to be' and warned 'there will be stumbles.' But

---

[39] Because this book deals with end-times prophecy, you may think it odd that I predict something 400 years out. But the Bible assures us that people will exist on earth 400 years in the future. Based on the signs of the times, I would guess that 400 years will place us in the millennial reign of Christ. I have no doubt the people of that age will view our science as primitive.

he assured 'science and scientists' would lead the way."[40]

If science and scientists are leading the way, then why do we need Biden? Why not cut out the middleman and put the technocrats directly in charge? Let me tell you why. Because a leader's job is about more than mathematics. Surely President Biden would overrule science if it directly violated his core moral beliefs. Wouldn't he?

The Moral Decision

Suppose a group of scientists were to tell the president that earth's resources will only be sustainable if he trims the planetary population down to a billion people. Suppose they say it is an emergency and he better do it quickly — as in this year. What would he do?

Don't dismiss this as impossible conjecture. Reputable scientists have come close to such claims many times. In 2015, Pope Francis published an encyclical on equity and climate change known as *Laudato si'*. A team of advisors helped him. His team included a surprising choice — Hans Joachim Schellnhuber, Director of the Potsdam Institute for Climate Impact Research.

Placing Schellnhuber on the pope's team shocked Catholics. The man had taken many public stands flatly contrary to the basic precepts of the Catholic faith. He was a well-known advocate of abortion and population control. He stated clearly and specifically that the planet's "carrying capacity" is "below one billion people."

---

[40] "Biden proposes a science-led New Deal to end pandemic suffering" by Jon Cohen and Meredith Wadman, *Science*, January 2021.

Schellnhuber has not called for the world's governments to kill off the excess. But he obviously sees a population now passing 8 billion people (as of 2023) as dangerous, perhaps catastrophic. He's not alone among radical environmentalists. *Investor's Business Daily* wrote, "Big Green believes too many human beings are the basic global problem. People, according to this view, are resource destroyers. Climate change, they say, is due to overpopulation of Mother Earth."[41]

According to the Australian Academy of Science, "The majority of studies estimate that the Earth's capacity is at or beneath 8 billion people."[42] According to these studies, the human race has already crossed earth's red line. Others, such as Schellnhuber, believe we passed it long ago.

Do We Really Want to Put Science in Charge?

What if a new wave of data (or a new fashion in thought) indicates an urgent need to reduce the planetary population to one billion? It is a hypothetical question, but a crucial one. How should the president respond? Should he "follow the science"? Perhaps he could start a nuclear war. Maybe he could send out a biological superweapon designed to genetically target and kill certain "undesirable" subgroups of humanity.

It is difficult to imagine Joe Biden cold-bloodedly killing billions of people. But it's easy to imagine a movement rising that would dedicate itself to harsh and radical methods of de-

---

[41] "Snow: Who's advising pope on climate?" by Catherine Snow, *The Detroit News*, July 10, 2015.

[42] "How many people can Earth actually support" an undated article featured on the Australian Academy of Science website.

population. It's easy to imagine because we've seen such people before.

"Dispassionate" scientists — the kind of technocrats so many futurists believe should be put in charge of everything — can be myopic. They often see the importance of their own specialty superseding all else. The dispassionate expert might tell us what's best for the world in his or her own specialty. But a dispassionate solution to one set of problems can easily turn into an impassioned disaster everywhere else.

In his famous farewell address, President Dwight Eisenhower did not just warn about "the military-industrial complex." He also warned about the "scientific-technological elite." He said, "It is the task of statesmanship to mold, to balance, and to integrate these and other forces, new and old, within the principles of our democratic system."

Experts disagree. Laymen decide. And that's the way it has to be.

PART THREE

Disaster Ahead

PART THREE: DISASTER AHEAD

CHAPTER 10

Paradise Through Unity

World War I hit utopian dreams hard. World War II seemed to destroy them altogether. The Nazi eugenics debacle placed radical solutions for "people of the Abyss" on the backburner. But world government got a shot in the arm. People stopped seeing peace as a lofty, far-off goal. It now took on the urgency of a fight for the survival of civilization. Increasingly, world leaders saw global governance as the only way to ensure peace.

President Woodrow Wilson called World War I "the war that will end war" — a phrase he borrowed directly from H. G. Wells.

Franklin Roosevelt would not use that phrase about World War II. But he clearly held a similar hope. FDR is the one who had put into motion the atomic bomb's development. And he had a good idea of its ramifications for future war. He spent much of the second World War laying the groundwork for what he dubbed "the United Nations." If he could make the UN powerful enough, he believed it would end most wars before they started.

Peace on Earth?

On June 26, 1945, 50 countries signed the UN Charter. The organization officially came into existence in October of that year — six months after FDR's death and only two months after the end of World War II. But it did not become the strong force FDR envisioned.

The Soviet Union had cooperated with the west during the war, and FDR hoped the cooperation would continue. But it didn't. Instead, the postwar world split into two camps — the United States and its allies versus the Soviet Union and its allies. They all joined the United Nations, but in most respects, the organization was a sham. The five permanent members of the UN Security Council, including the United States and Soviet Union, held the real power. Any of the five nations could veto anything meaningful that may not align with their interests. This division between communism and the "free world" made the United Nations a paper tiger.

Their enmity made another world war seem inevitable. But events were afoot that also made it unthinkable.

Truman and the Bomb

Roosevelt died without ever letting Harry Truman know about the Manhattan Project's ongoing attempt to develop an atomic bomb. Truman learned about it on April 25, 1945, his 12th day as president. Secretary of Defense Stimson started the meeting by handing Truman a memo. It began:

PART THREE: DISASTER AHEAD

Within four months we shall in all probability have completed the most terrible weapon ever known in human history, one bomb of which could destroy a whole city.

From the beginning, American officials understood the bomb's world-changing implications. Truman said later that when giving him the briefing, Stimson "seemed as concerned with the role of the atomic bomb in shaping history as in its capacity to shorten the war."[43]

The first successful test of a nuclear weapon occurred at 5:29 AM, July 16, 1945, at Trinity Site in New Mexico. It occurred on the same day Truman toured Berlin's bombed out ruins during the Potsdam Conference with Stalin and Churchill.[44] Secretary of Defense Stimson broke the news to Churchill. "Stimson, what was gunpowder?" Churchill asked rhetorically. "What was electricity? Meaningless. This atomic bomb is the Second Coming in wrath."

Between sessions at Potsdam, Truman walked across the room to talk privately with Joseph Stalin. He remembered it like this. "I casually mentioned to Stalin that we had a new weapon of unusual destructive force. All he said was that he was glad to hear it and hoped we would make 'good use of it against the Japanese.'"

Members of Truman's inner circle could not hear the conversation, but they knew what Truman was telling Stalin. The Soviet leader's nonchalant reaction stunned them. They thought he must not have understood the significance of what he just

---

[43] *Truman* by David McCullough, Simon & Schuster, 1992.

[44] Churchill would lose his bid to remain the UK Prime Minister while at Potsdam and would be replaced by the new PM, Clement Attlee.

heard. But he did understand. He knew all about the Manhattan Project. His nonchalance and lack of curiosity foretold a great darkness coming upon the earth.

The Prophesied Fire of Destruction

David McCullough's *Truman* biography explains, "The fact was Stalin already knew more than any of the Americans or British imagined. Soviet nuclear research had begun in 1942, and as would be learned later, a German-born physicist at Los Alamos, a naturalized British citizen named Klaus Fuchs, had been supplying the Russians with atomic secrets for some time, information that in Moscow was judged 'extremely excellent and very valuable.' Stalin had understood perfectly what Truman said. Later, in the privacy of their Babelsberg quarters, according to Marshal Georgi Zhukov, Stalin instructed Molotov to 'tell Kurchatov [of the Soviet atomic project] to hurry up the work.'"[45]

The possibility of quickly ending the war with Japan exhilarated Truman. But the tool they would use horrified him. "We have discovered the most terrible bomb in the history of the world," Truman wrote in his diary the day he ordered the Air Force to proceed with the plan.

"'Terrible' was the word he would keep coming back to," McCullough wrote. "He wondered if the bomb might be 'the fire of destruction' prophesied in the Bible."[46]

On August 6, 1945, the United States dropped an atomic bomb codenamed "Little Boy" on the city of Hiroshima, Japan.

---

[45] *Truman* by David McCullough, Simon & Schuster, 1992.
[46] Ibid.

PART THREE: DISASTER AHEAD

Truman, on a ship headed back to the US after the Potsdam conference, sent out a message to his countrymen. "Sixteen hours ago an American airplane dropped one bomb on Hiroshima.... It is an atomic bomb. It is a harnessing of the basic power of the universe."

Three days later, the United States dropped a second atomic bomb, this one on the Japanese city of Nagasaki. Both bombs proved deadlier and more devastating than their inventors dared hope. Japan soon surrendered. The rest of the world celebrated, but a nuclear cloud hung over the festivities.

Fear of Armageddon

On August 7th, Hanson Baldwin of *The New York Times*, wrote, "Yesterday we clinched victory in the Pacific, but we sowed the whirlwind."

The *Kansas City Star* said, "We are dealing with an invention that could overwhelm civilization."

The *St. Louis Post-Dispatch* warned that science might have just "signed the mammalian world's death warrant and deeded an earth in ruins to the ants."

Fear of utter destruction loomed over the world. People wanted peace and safety so once again, a familiar message will rise to popularity.

One World or None

Many of the scientists who worked on the bomb felt great remorse. That year, 1945, a group of Manhattan Project scientists founded the "Bulletin of the Atomic Scientists." In 1947, they began publishing their famous Doomsday Clock. 1945 also marked the formation of "The Federation of American Scientists."

In 1946, the latter group sponsored a short film entitled, *One World or None*. It gives graphic details of what they then understood about the horrors of atomic war. It concludes by saying:

> *It is therefore an imperative necessity that all the nations of the world unite to avert catastrophe. The United Nations must establish a worldwide control of atomic energy and of other weapons of mass destruction. Representatives of the peoples of the world must together make laws which will abolish war, laws which will hold the individual in all lands responsible for crime against world peace.... The choice is clear. It is life or death.*[47] *(Emphasis added.)*

Control over all nuclear weapons would have instantly given the United Nations the most powerful military force on earth. In other words, they were calling for a one-world government with the power to annihilate anything that stood in its way. To President Truman, the idea was unthinkable. He trusted the US, its people and Constitution, over the UN.

An End to National Sovereignty

The Federation of American Scientists released a companion book with the same title and the same one-world govern-

---

[47] *One World or None*, directed by Philip Ragan, narrated by Raymond Swing, Philip Ragan Productions, presented by the National Committee on Atomic Information, 1946.

ment emphasis.[48] Some of the most famous and influential people of the era wrote chapters. They included Albert Einstein, Robert Oppenheimer, and Walter Lippmann. The book made it clear that atomic weapons terrified these people and would likely result in the end of the world. As with Nimrod and his proclamation to provide peace and safety through the construction of the Tower of Babel, we once again see the most respected scientific and political minds of the 20th century echoing the same message — with the threat of annihilation, only a world government can save humanity.

The small size of nuclear weapons relative to their explosive yield frightened Edward Condon, a nuclear physicist from the Manhattan Project. He wrote about the possibility of nuclear weapons in the hands of terrorists or saboteurs. With the arrival of suitcase-sized nuclear devices and the worldwide war on terror, his concerns seem especially prescient today.

Condon saw only one hope — "international control of atomic energy. The saboteur cannot be found, but the factory that makes his bomb need never exist."[49]

Niels Bohr was a Nobel Prize winning physicist whose discoveries made atomic bombs possible. He wrote, "The fate of humanity will depend on its ability to unite in averting common dangers.... Such measures will, of course, demand the abolition of barriers hitherto considered necessary to safeguard national interests."[50]

---

[48] *One World or None: A Report to the Public on the Full Meaning of the Atomic Bomb*, edited by Dexter Masters, Editor of Science Illustrated, and Katharine Way of the Metallurgical Laboratory, University of Chicago. Authors include Albert Einstein, and J. R. Oppenheimer, McGraw-Hill Book Company, 1946.

[49] Ibid.

[50] Ibid.

What "barriers" were "hitherto considered necessary to safeguard national interests"? They would include a nation's sovereignty over its own laws and borders. In other words, his call for the end of these "barriers" meant the end of nation-states as they have historically been defined. The countries of old would lose their traditional standing in favor of a new, global entity.

These voices echo to us today from the 1940s. But their influence continues. Ask yourself this. Are borders more meaningful today, or less? With every treaty, supranational organizations take more of the power once reserved to nations. Their dreams have been a long time coming, but they are important because they are upon right now.

Global Control of Individuals

Walter Lippmann has been called "the most influential journalist of the 20th century,"[51] and the "Father of Modern Journalism."[52] He argued that international law as it had previously been practiced, would not have the strength to confront the nuclear danger.

Sovereign states, he contended, could not effectively hold one another responsible for the treaties they signed. "Why not?" he asked. "Because the remedy is as bad as the disease: the peaceable nations have to be willing to wage total war in order to prevent total war. The remedy is so crude, so expensive, and usually so repulsive, that it will not be applied by the very peo-

---

[51] "Walter Lippmann and American journalism today" by Sidney Blumenthal, openDemocracy, October 31, 2007.

[52] *The Filter Bubble: How the New Personalized Web Is Changing What We Read and How We Think* by Eli Pariser, Penguin Books, 2011.

ples who are supposed to apply it, namely by the peace-loving peoples."[53]

The public in those days well understood this argument. World War I ended with the Treaty of Versailles. Hitler came to power, Germany acted as if the treaty never existed. Hitler reoccupied territories Germany was supposed to have given up and began illegally rearming the nation. Other countries did not see these things as worth going to war over, so they let him continue until it was too late.

Lippmann believed that treaties between nations would always be weak if there had been no enforcement mechanism short of war. But Lippmann saw hope in the Nuremberg Trials of Nazi war criminals. The trials did not aim at holding a nation accountable for its actions, but individuals accountable for theirs.

Lippmann saw this as the blueprint for a successful world government. Another set of agreements between nations, he felt, could not be effective by themselves. He believed world government must make laws that reach past old national sovereignties all the way to individual people. He believed it necessary to create international law with power over the citizens of previously sovereign nations. "If mankind is to rely upon obedience to the law by such a multitude of individuals, the rules agreed upon must become the supreme law in all lands, and all previous and subsequent national law must conform to the world law."

The crux of the argument is that real power means direct control over individuals. You do not really have charge of the world until you have charge of its people... as in "that no one

---

[53] Ibid.

may buy or sell except one who has the mark."[54]

Central power over the world's individuals proved a bridge too far for post-World War II planners. But soon, there would exist a shortcut to the domination of the individual being made possible by new technologies that are now coming to complete fruition. The coming one world government, and later the Antichrist, will seize control of individuals by taking charge of their money. Control a person's money, and you own him head-to-toe. But for such a person to control such a system, there must be a demand for such a leader.

The Leadership Vacuum

What I am about to say is not about politics. It is a factual report on the condition of the world at this moment in history. I write these words in the year of our Lord 2023, and I write with deep concern for what they portend.

From Australia to Asia to Africa to Europe to the Americas, the world is suffering from a leadership vacuum. Today's leaders tend to be weak and spiritually small men and women, without vision and with little charisma. I know that is a sweeping statement and a subjective one. But I think most people in most countries agree with me.

For a long time, China's Xi was considered a strong leader, an iron man. But he has lately been leading his country to the brink of catastrophe. His rule seems more and more about staying in power rather than his nation's success. In fact, he looks smaller by the day. He's become a mere bomb thrower — searching out and supporting evil regimes like Russia, North Korea, and Iran.

---

[54] Revelation 13:17

PART THREE: DISASTER AHEAD

Vladimir Putin once seemed like an amoral pragmatist who at least held Russia in a firm grip. Today that grip has slipped. His nonsensical war with Ukraine showed his country's military — once vaunted and feared — to be weak, poorly trained, and badly led. He's been killing his enemies for a long time. Now he also kills his friends. He's like an old man moving slowly in a walker, cursing the children who play nearby.

Do you remember British Prime Minister Boris Johnson? He led the Conservative Party, but he lived in #10 Downing Street like a frat boy on holiday. Liz Truss replaced him. She aspired to be like her hero, Margaret Thatcher. If only! She came across as a woman who would struggle to lead a class of 3rd graders. Her 50-day tenure as Prime Minister was the shortest in UK history. As I write this, her replacement, Rishi Sunak, hasn't had time to build much of a track record. Still, first impressions indicate a man completely lacking in the kind of gravitas now needed.

Boris Johnson's lack of sober leadership seems typical of the era. Look at Finland's Prime Minister, 36-year-old Sanna Marin. She seems more intent on dirty dancing with her friends than on leading her nation through this time of turmoil.

Maybe I'm wrong about some of these. I'm giving impressions gleaned from a faraway country. But in leadership, impressions count!

Do I need to mention Joe Biden, Justin Trudeau, or Emmanuel Macron? In a September 2022 interview on CNN, Jake Tapper asked President Macron of France if he's worried about American democracy. Macron answered, "I worry about all of us." He went on to say, "I think we have [a] big crisis of democracies."

Part of the crisis is a vacuum of leadership. When President Biden spoke to the United Nations in 2022, he scowled, he lectured, and he spoke every word in apparent anger. None but the most partisan could look at that speech and see leadership or persuasion. It looked dull, flat, and desperate. He looked like a shrimp of a boy trying (and failing) to appear strong in the presence of a perceived bully. He exhibited only the passions of fear, frustration, irritation, and sanctimoniousness.

I'm not talking here about the political positions held by these politicians. Some are pretty bad, but that's not my point. In the United States, we have had many presidents with whom I vehemently disagreed politically, but whose leadership abilities I admired. This is about a stunning void of leadership and persuasiveness.

Of course, the leaders of the world may not recognize their own shortcomings, but eventually, when a one world government is in place, the elites will come to realize that true global peace and control cannot be accomplished through majority votes by democratically appointed leaders. The need for a benevolent ruler, an elite among elites, will be recognized.

Voids tend to be filled. And I believe this one soon will be — by the worst monster in human history.

PART THREE: DISASTER AHEAD

CHAPTER 11

The Problem with People

Klaus Schwab, Founder and Executive Chairman of the World Economic Forum addressed the opening session of the World Government Summit in Dubai. "History is slowly at a turning point," he said. "We do not know the full extent of the systematic and structural changes that will happen, but we do know that energy systems, supply chains and food systems will be deeply affected."

Mr. Schwab is telling the truth when he says he does not know "the full extent of the systematic and structural changes that will happen." At this point in world history, few do. <u>Those who best understand history's present trajectory are those who use the Bible as their source of such knowledge.</u>

Cogs on Gears Within Sprockets Turning Wheels

The C. S. Lewis novel, *That Hideous Strength*, depicts circles within circles of a satanic plot to control the world. Characters who believe they see themselves as insiders are often far on the outside, with no knowledge of the actual agenda. Early on, the story's gullible young male protagonists, Mark Studdock, encounters Lord Feverstone, a powerful member of the global cabal.

Until this meeting, Studdock saw two figures in the local college — Curry, the Sub-warden, and James Busby, the Bursar — as the ultimate insiders in the most desirable of cliques. It stuns Mark to see Feverstone bait them, and even make fun of them. After they have gone, Feverstone says to Studdock, "Our two poor friends, though they can be persuaded to take the right train, or even to drive it, haven't a ghost of a notion where it's going to, or why."[55]

The story sweeps young Studdock into deeper and darker inner circles. He eventually finds that Feverstone himself is not fully on the inside. Schwab and his ilk are mostly like Curry and Busby — enthusiastically "pushing the envelope" with only vague and superficial notions where they're pushing it. But even in ignorance, Schwab and friends are fully onboard the train they're helping to drive.

Most of them have not yet recognized their real master, or the extent of his evil intentions. But they long for power and no longer trust democracy. The problem they see with democracy is people. Therefore, they believe a small group of enlightened

---

[55] *That Hideous Strength* by C. S. Lewis, published by The Bodley Head, 1945.

individuals must take charge of humanity before humanity destroys itself or makes earth uninhabitable. That's what the World Economic Forum is — elites planning the future of the world; elites deciding for us all.

Man Taking Charge of Man

Today, the list of things that scare the elite is longer than it was in the days of H. G. Wells. Today's world-planners want to wean us off meat, especially red meat. They fear that cow burps wreak great harm on earth's atmosphere. They fret over aerosol sprays, baby diapers, and SUVs.

In places where regular people can afford cars, they love their gasoline-fueled freedom. They drive all over the place. World-planners want to wean us off cars completely, but first they will switch us to electric cars. Science — actual science — does not yet fully know the long-term environmental effects of so-called Zero Emissions Vehicles (ZEVs) and their batteries.

Elite thinkers see plastic straws and grocery bags as big problems, but the masses keep on using them unless forced to stop. It's telling that they can get people to vote against free plastic grocery bags. Those same people could have stopped using them at any time before passing such a law, but they did not. Then, when forced to use heavy reusable plastic bags, they forget to reuse them. They pay their dimes to buy new ones on most trips to the store, and wind up polluting the environment with thicker plastic bags not designed to disintegrate in a landfill.

Elites also believe that in a fit of patriotic fervor, we-the-people might start a nuclear war.

They see humanity itself as dangerous and unpredictable, and they have a point. Mobs do crazy things. People get silly notions in their heads. But so do dictators, popes, and academics. <u>Humanity taking charge of humanity does not answer the problem</u>. It pushes it from the many to the few. This may make us even more vulnerable. The few have just as much potential for foolishness and corruption — yet with less accountability.

C. S. Lewis's Lord Feverstone brings us to the world-planners' ugly, but inevitable conclusion.

> *"Man has got to take charge of man. That means, remember, that some men have got to take charge of the rest—which is another reason for cashing in on it as soon as one can. You and I want to be the people who do the taking charge, not the ones who are taken charge of."*

The Global Authority

Catholic theologians have traditionally held to something called "subsidiarity." Dictionary.com defines it as, "In the Roman Catholic Church a principle of social doctrine that all social bodies exist for the sake of the individual so that what individuals are able to do, society should not take over, and what small societies can do, larger societies should not take over."

That idea expresses something Americans have long held to as a governing principle. Where possible, let people govern themselves. Otherwise, keep government as close to the individual as possible. A nearby government better understands the individual and can better respond to the individual's needs. A big national government is necessary for things like the common defense, but we also need our village councils.

Though a Catholic concept, popes don't always agree. In his 1963 encyclical, *Pacem in Terris* (Peace on Earth), John XXIII called for increased world government. He referred to it as a "general authority equipped with world-wide power." He explained, "The universal common good presents us with problems which are world-wide in their dimensions; problems, therefore, which cannot be solved except by a public authority with power, organization and means co-extensive with these problems, and with a world-wide sphere of activity. Consequently the moral order itself demands the establishment of some such general form of public authority."

In a 2009 encyclical, Pope Benedict cited John XXIII in calling for a "world political authority." Such an authority could protect poorer nations and "manage the global economy… to bring about integral and timely disarmament, food security and peace; to guarantee the protection of the environment and to regulate migration: for all this, there is urgent need of a true world political authority."[56]

One Authoritative Source

In his 2015 encyclical on climate change, Pope Francis took that idea even further. He repeatedly expressed his distrust of democracy. "International negotiations," he wrote, "cannot make significant progress due to positions taken by countries which place their national interests above the global common good."

He complained that nations and people in general act in their own best interests. He saw that as a problem. He called for the nations of the world to set up "global regulatory norms… to

---

[56] "Caritas in veritate" ("Charity in truth") Encyclical of Pope Benedict XVI, 2009.

impose obligations and prevent unacceptable actions."

Over the half-century between these encyclicals, there seems to be a growing disdain for democracy. Pope Francis wrote, "There is urgent need of a true world political authority…. One authoritative source of oversight and coordination… which lays down rules for admissible conduct in the light of the common good."

But even "a true world political authority" might change over time if its power is subject to the people's will expressed through their votes. Aware of the "danger," Francis wrote, "Continuity is essential, because policies related to climate change and environmental protection cannot be altered with every change of government."

You see the problem. People worry about their next paycheck or their next meal. Their votes reflect these immediate concerns. But world-planners, whether in the ivory towers of American universities or the papal throne in the Holy See, fear the immediacy of democracy. The mob might burn the world with burping cows as they attempt to feed their young.

So why would people put up with government stripping them of their rights and their power? Simple. They are educated to believe that democracy and capitalism lead to racism, unfairness, and destruction of the planet.

You may believe these sentiments have been adopted by a radical minority, but consider that as of 2023, the medium age of one living on the earth is 30 years old. Someone who was born into the Millennial generation, is now 27 to 42 years of age. Of course, the following generations seem to have only amplified the Millennials in the fears and ideologies of global warming and socialism. That means the world's elites have already educated the majority of the world's population with the before-mentioned beliefs. In fact, the majority of those 42 years old and younger almost certainly see your views and fears regarding a one world government as mere conspiracy theory. Ironically, it's their lack of their critical thinking that will usher in the end of the world as we know it — giving rise to the Antichrist and his Mark. But we'll talk about this a little later.

MARKING THE MASSES

PART THREE: DISASTER AHEAD

CHAPTER 12

The Open Conspiracy

The word "conspire" carries an implication of "secrecy." Dictionary.com says, *"Conspire* commonly means to secretly plan with multiple other people to do something wrong, evil, or illegal."

We can quickly dismiss most conspiracy theories because human beings talk a lot. We seem hardwired to tell secrets — at least other people's secrets. The more people a conspiracy involves, the less likely it can remain hidden. Human nature is what it is. People tell secrets — the bigger and juicier the better.

H. G. Wells told of another kind of conspiracy — an "open conspiracy." This means a group of people working at least partially in the open for a goal that is not hidden. Because it is open, there are no limits to its size.

Happily for me, no one can call me a "conspiracy nut" for pointing out an "open conspiracy." It doesn't creep forth from the dark corners of my imagination. It stands in the open for all to see. Look at "The Great Reset." Is it a conspiracy theory? No. It is an open movement started by Klaus Schwab and supported by global influencers in the World Economic Forum. As Klaus Schwab said when he opened the World Economic Forum in 2020, "Change can be shaped by us."

A Federal Government of All Humankind

In *The Open Conspiracy*, Wells presented his plan for bringing about world government. He called his book "a sort of provisional 'Bible.'" He predicted a world "politically, socially, and economically unified." Over time, details change, but the central goal stays the same. Wells called it a conspiracy toward a "world commonweal." Today, we would say, "world commonwealth," meaning a world federation of states.

"The Open Conspiracy," Wells said, "is not necessarily antagonistic to any existing government…. It does not want to destroy existing controls and forms of human association, but either to supersede or amalgamate them into a common world directorate. If constitutions, parliaments, and kings can be dealt with as provisional institutions, trustees for the coming of age of the world commonweal, and in so far as they are conducted in that spirit, the Open Conspiracy makes no attack upon them."[57]

In other words, if a nation submits its sovereignty to the new world government, it will not be crushed.

An organization pressing for world government today is "Citizens for Global Solutions." They say, "We envision a federal government of all humankind that unites the nations and all

---

[57] *The Open Conspiracy: Blue Prints for a World Revolution* by H. G. Wells, published by Gollancz, 1928.

citizens of the world under a constitution built on the principles followed by the United States and other great nations."

Compare this vision to "subsidiarity." Government works best when it is small enough to recognize individuals, knowing when it should render aid and when it should get out of the way. The bigger and farther away the government, the more it sees people as mere abstractions.

Swallowing Up the World

Wells said the movement "will be frankly a world religion... definitely and obviously attempting to swallow up the entire population of the world."

It's interesting that the logical causality of a one world government establishing a superseding and enforced global religion is precisely what the Bible prophesies will occur at the end of days. The Book of Revelation clearly depicts that a global religion with be spearheaded by a religious leader known as The False Prophet who enforces worship of the Antichrist above all else. If you're not a part of the system, then you're against it.

> *"He was granted power to give breath to the image of the beast, that the image of the beast should both speak and cause as many as would not worship the image of the beast to be killed."*
>
> *— Revelation 13:15*

Later, H.G Wells said, "All these obsolete values and attitudes with which our minds are cumbered must be cleared out if the new faith is to have free play. We have to clear them out not only from our own minds but from the minds of others who are to become our associates. The finer and more picturesque these obsolescent loyalties, obsolescent standards of honour, obsolescent religious associations, may seem to us, the more thoroughly must we seek to release our minds and the minds of those about us from them and cut off all thought of a return."

He believed that the "finer and more picturesque" the old ideas, "the more thoroughly" they must be resisted. Nothing is "finer or more picturesque" than Jesus and His gospel. Resisters, he said, would be "vestiges of the ancient order." These would come, he predicted, from traditional religious faiths, especially Christianity. He emphasized that, "We cannot compromise with these."

He called for world biological and population controls, giving a minimum standard of freedom and welfare. Wells said the new world order would replace private ownership with "a responsible world directorate serving the common ends of the race."

An End to Private Ownership

In 2016, the World Economic Forum produced a video giving predictions about the world in 2030. One of those predictions said, "You'll own nothing. And you'll be happy. What you want you'll rent, and it'll be delivered by drone."

Some have twisted the quote, but its implications are still staggering. Owning nothing, depending on drones to bring us what we need as we need it, leaves people and nations vulnerable to supply chain disruptions and power-hungry politicians. Klaus Schwab loves to talk about "stakeholders," and their importance to world planning and world governing. He should remember that when people own nothing, they stop feeling like

PART THREE: DISASTER AHEAD

stakeholders.

Ownership stands as a powerful barrier against slavery.

'Imagine No Possessions'

During the days of Covid lockdown, the face of Wonder Woman appeared on screens around the world. She had come to save the day, or at least provide a little lockdown entertainment. Gal Gadot portrayed the big screen version of Wonder Woman in several films. She gathered some friends on social media and they sang.

Oddly enough, the actress with a net worth estimated at $30 million[58], chose a song promoting socialism — John Lennon's "Imagine." Lennon himself was an extremely wealthy man, but he called his song "anti-capitalistic." His widow, Yoko Ono, has a net worth estimated at $700 million.[59]

The song has become an anthem among the world's elite. They use it regularly at the Olympics and for other global gatherings. Despite its implication that religious faith causes war and should be done away with, they sometimes even use it as a Christmas carol.

In the song, John Lennon imagines a world without war. That's a pleasant thought. Most of us despise war. But Lennon's *means* to peace is the removal of human meaning. He wrote, "Imagine there's no Heaven . . . No hell . . . No countries . . . Nothing to kill or die for. And no religion too."[60]

---

[58] Source: celebritynetworth.com, in October 2022.

[59] Ibid.

[60] "Imagine" by John Lennon, Downtown Music Publishing, 1971

Think about the words, "Nothing to kill or die for."[61] He's imagining a dark and ugly world spiraling in on itself — a world where nothing holds enough value for you to risk your life — "nothing... to die for." He imagined a world where nothing holds greater importance than one's own life. Think about the emptiness of a world with nothing that's greater than yourself.

When Lennon wrote the song, he was already the father of one son, and would later father another. If an intruder came into his home threatening his child, wouldn't he have risked his life if it meant saving his child? In a world with nothing worth dying for, then life itself — the thing he's trying to preserve — loses meaning. In imagining a world with "Nothing to kill or die for," he's also imagined a world with nothing to live for.

A Spoonful of Sugar

In the Geoffrey Giuliano book, *Lennon in America*, John described "Imagine" as "anti-religious, anti-nationalistic, anti-conventional, anti-capitalistic... but because it's sugar-coated, it's accepted."[62]

If "Imagine" ranks as one of your favorites, I hope I'm not offending you. I understand the tremendous beauty in the song's haunting melody. It really is a masterpiece of popular music. It is also an anthem to nihilism — sad, dark, and ugly — attempting to take humanity back to its origins in the dust.

Yet, according to one poll on the Canadian Broadcasting

---

[61] Ibid.

[62] *Lennon in America* by Geoffrey Giuliano, Cooper Square Press, 2000.

Corporation, it is the greatest song of the last 100 years.[63] Imagine that.

Former President Jimmy Carter has said, "In many countries around the world — my wife and I have visited about 125 countries — you hear John Lennon's song 'Imagine' used almost equally with national anthems."

The song calls for an end to borders and nations, implying the need for a single world state. It calls for an end to capitalism and religious faith. When sung publicly, it evokes tears of devotion. How ironic that a song making the end of religion into the beginning of hope, evokes feelings of religious mysticism and devotion.

People may not be thinking actively of the words or their implications. But they mean it when they sing, "I hope someday you'll join us, and the world will live as one."[64]

That — is an open conspiracy! *[handwritten: SATANIC INSPIRED LERICS]*

Kumbaya Without the Prayer

Today, world government remains an open conspiracy. It does not require thousands of people to keep a secret. Just the opposite. Millions of people openly support it. They may have secret meetings in which the immediate strategy may be briefly hidden, but there can be no secret about the purposed intent. Total and uncompromising control.

In his autobiography, *Walter Cronkite: A Reporter's Life*, Cronkite wrote, "The proud nations someday will see the light

---

[63] *Still the Greatest: The Essential Songs of the Beatles' Solo Careers* by Andrew Grant Jackson, Scarecrow Press, 2012.

[64] Ibid.

and, for the common good and their own survival, yield up their precious sovereignty, just as America's thirteen colonies did two centuries ago." He then wrote that we will eventually "come to our senses and establish a world executive and a parliament of nations."[65]

Like Cronkite, most globalists see their cause as the natural outgrowth of fundamental, even noble desires. They want siblinghood, peace, and equity for all living things, including the human populations of all nations. It's Kumbaya without the prayer.

History tells a different story. Those who have come closest to the realization of the globalist dream have had a different motive — power. Napoleon, Alexander, and Nebuchadnezzar are among the most famous. Each of them rose to power by the strategic use of power. They forced unity over a significant portion of the earth — not because of unity's warmth and fuzziness, but because unity amplified their power.

Today, idealistic foot soldiers across the world are working hard to bring about a global government. Many of them see it as a worthy and necessary goal. But ultimately, it's still all about the accumulation of human power. And it will one day facilitate a final great rebellion against God.

Most globalists are not stupid; they are afraid. Some might think of them as James Bond villains plotting to take over the world. But real globalists are often highly motivated and idealistic. They look at it almost like a mathematical formula. If the world had one government, everyone would be on the same side. There would be no one to fight... except perhaps Klingons.

---

[65] *Walter Cronkite: A Reporter's Life* by Walter Cronkite, Alfred A. Knopf, 1996.

PART THREE: DISASTER AHEAD

Teeth

That Hideous Strength, by C. S. Lewis, gives us a powerful insight. Curry, Busby, Feverstone, and Studdock discuss a coming evil organization N.I.C.E. (National Institute of Co-ordinated Experiments). Each explains what he thinks makes the Institute significant. Busby talks about the size and scope of the operation, the size of the facilities, and the huge number of people involved. He mentions that it will have its own police force. Lord Feverstone, in a mocking voice says he has heard that, "the sanitation of the Institute was going to be something quite out of the ordinary."

The first two men feel they are being mocked and point out that sanitation is important. Curry tells them about a new device, the "Pragmatometer," that will allow the scientists from all fields to coordinate their work instantly.

Finally, Feverstone asks Mark Studdock his opinion. "'I think,' said Mark, 'that James touched on the most important point when he said that it would have its own legal staff and its own police. I don't give a fig for Pragmatometers and sanitation. The real thing is that this time we're going to get science applied to social problems and backed by the whole force of the state, just as war has been backed by the whole force of the state in the past. One hopes, of course, that it'll find out more than the old free-lance science did: but what's certain is that it can do more.'"

Later, when they were alone, Feverstone tells Mark that he understood the point. Science is powerful when the people with guns back it up. Apparently, that's also how Walter Cronkite saw it. He wanted a world government "with a legislature, executive and judiciary, and police to enforce its international laws and keep the peace."

The idea of a global ideology that can be enforced across borders through superseding international law is terrifying, but this is precisely what we know will happen. The prophet Daniel warned us of this precise authority that will be yielded by the coming one world government.

> *"After this I saw in the night visions, and behold, a fourth beast, dreadful and terrible, exceedingly strong. It had huge iron teeth; it was devouring, breaking in pieces, and trampling the residue with its feet. It was different from all the beasts that were before it, and it had ten horns."*
>
> — *Daniel 7:7*

World Federalist Movement

Cronkite was a member of the World Federalist Movement. At one time or another, the group included such luminaries as Albert Einstein, Mahatma Gandhi, Martin Luther King Jr., Peter Ustinov, 1940 Republican nominee for President Wendell Willkie, *Stuart Little* and *Charlotte's Web* author E. B. White, and a host of other notable world figures from a variety of backgrounds and occupations.

These were not stupid or mean people. I'm sure that when asked, they gave noble reasons for joining the movement. Most, I think, would say that world federalism was human civilization's last great hope of survival.

But a unified world needs a unifying force.

PART THREE: DISASTER AHEAD

Democracy Acts Up... Again

Walter Cronkite called members of the post-World War I US Senate, "American chauvinists, blindly jealous of meaningless sovereignty, rejected Wilson's dream of a League of Nations, a mild first step toward world government."[66]

Like most globalists, Cronkite imagined global government working as a democracy very much like that of the United States. Yet he derided the results of that democracy. He called the elected officials who refused to ratify the League of Nations "chauvinists." In a single nation — a place where people mostly held similar views — the people's representatives could not agree on something Cronkite saw as crucial. This again calls democracy itself into question — especially a global democracy.

This also calls into question his claim that national sovereignty is "meaningless." In the US, it was meaningful enough to reject the League of Nations.

The post-World War II nations were also unwilling to give up any real sovereignty to the United Nations. Consider the problem. We've all seen how difficult democracy can be with only three people in the room. For a city or state, it becomes dramatically more complicated. The larger the nation, the more regions it will have. Where there are greater varieties of speech, culture, and thought, things become increasingly chaotic.

Now bring representatives of all nations and all cultures into one room. It becomes practically impossible. Anyone who expects the world's nations to govern together harmoniously and democratically will be disappointed. In other words, the pursuit of an effective democratic one world government will

---

[66] Ibid.

inevitably lead to the realization that a ruling individual at the top is needed.

The impossibility of a truly democratic world government has not been lost on global elites. They do not intend to allow the unwashed masses sovereignty over the planet. They will make a nod to democratic principles, but the world they plan would be run by elites for elites.

Make no mistake. Although public perception may appear that many elites' intentions are to end war and ushering in an age of financial and social stability (peace and safety), it's not the primary agenda, but rather the side effects that will benefit riff raff like you and me.

In fact, when Walter Cronkite was faced with this truth by an individual regarding Jesus Christ soon returning to rule and reign over the governments of the world, Mr. Cronkite lashed out, stating, "I am glad to sit at the right hand of Satan" in referencing that he and his ilk will bring about a real New World Order. Like Nimrod, the goal is not for the benefit of humankind, but rather the desire to replace God with Man to reap the full indulgence of earthy rewards.

Using the world's population is simply the means to an end to establish their perfect utopia. If the people are subdued and controlled, then the elites can have their paradise. Older generations may be set in their ways regarding God, family, and freedom, but the kids are primed to be molded into the very tools of change that the elites need. It's going to be the young generations of today that usher in a world you could never have imagined. It's our kids that will ultimately bring about the end of everything.

PART FOUR

Insanity by Design

MARKING THE MASSES

PART FOUR: INSANITY BY DESIGN

CHAPTER 13

The New Generations

Harmony Healthcare did a 2022 study involving more than 1,000 members of Gen Z, whom they defined as then including ages 18 to 24. They found that "42% have a diagnosed mental health condition." But that doesn't tell the real story because "57% are currently taking medication for their mental health condition."

Reported problems include anxiety, depression, ADHD, PTSD, OCD, eating disorders, bipolar disorder, borderline personality disorder, along with addiction and substance abuse. Isn't it time someone in our society pointed out the fact that what we're doing is not working?

The Kids

In late 2021, America received a dire warning about the state of its children's mental health. The American Academy of

Pediatrics, the Children's Hospital Association and the American Academy of Child and Adolescent Psychiatry sent out a joint statement declaring a national mental health crisis among children.

Media across the nation covered the story. They statement did not mention lack of discipline, the deterioration of families, a moral freefall, or any one of hundreds of other reasons for the mental health crisis among children. The statement said, "This worsening crisis in child and adolescent mental health is inextricably tied to the stress brought on by COVID-19 and the ongoing struggle for racial justice."

Kids are confused. They're being led young, hedonistic "influencers." Test scores keep dropping even as educators make "standardized" tests easier and easier. School shootings are up. Governments now spend vast sums of money retrofitting schools that were designed and built for a saner world. Political activists push the fear of school shootings onto the kids themselves. The trauma of schoolchildren has become a means of making a political point, and activists don't mind exacerbating that trauma when it benefits their cause.

Children live in fear of loud noises. Many can't play outside. They see strangers as an imminent threat against their lives. The media hypes stories to get viewers and internet clicks. Meanwhile, their excited exaggerations further terrorize the young. Schools tell kids that they are either oppressed victims or oppressors of victims. They pronounce guilt and innocence based on skin color.

Young people across the world are suffering.

PART FOUR: INSANITY BY DESIGN

Nightmare Minds

NPR wrote, "When it comes to suicide in particular, the groups point to data showing that by 2018, suicide was the second-leading cause of death for people between the ages of 10 and 24. Teenage girls have emerged particularly at risk. From February to March of 2022, emergency department visits for suspected suicide attempts were up 51% for girls ages 12 to 17, compared with the same period in 2019, according to data from the Centers for Disease Control and Prevention."[67]

In the same article, Dr. Gabrielle Carlson, president of the American Academy of Child and Adolescent Psychiatry elaborated on the situation. "We are caring for young people with soaring rates of depression, anxiety, trauma, loneliness, and suicidality that will have lasting impacts on them, their families, their communities, and all of our futures."

Her words sound nightmarish — "soaring rates of depression, anxiety, trauma, loneliness, and suicidality." If this is primarily a result of "the ongoing struggle for racial justice," why has it become worse? That struggle has been going on in America for hundreds of years. We must recognize that there is more to this than a set of leftwing talking points.

Several groups have proposed screenings for depression and suicide risk among children starting at age 10 or earlier. In October of 2022, the US Preventive Services Task Force recommended such screenings even for children who show no symptoms of a mental health problem.

---

[67] "Pediatricians say the mental health crisis among kids has become a national emergency" by Deepa Shivaram, National Public Radio, October 20, 2021.

But the screenings could be another problem. Will they design the tests to single out well-adjusted kids whose families happen to teach things they consider dangerous — like biblical morality?

Debased Minds

We start to understand the real problem by examining it in the light of Romans 1:28. "Even as they did not like to retain God in their knowledge, God gave them over to a debased mind, to do those things which are not fitting."

The word translated in the New King James as "debased mind," is translated "depraved mind" in the New American Standard Bible and "reprobate mind" in the King James Version. My friend Hal Lindsey is most famous as the author of *The Late Great Planet Earth*. He describes "a depraved mind" as "a mind so perverted it cannot think in its own best interest."[68] To the point where they reject all sense of morality; replaced entirely by insatiable desires and doing only what they deem right in their own eyes.

> *"Woe to those who call evil good, and good evil; Who put darkness for light, and light for darkness; Who put bitter for sweet, and sweet for bitter!"*
>
> *— Isaiah 5:20*

At first glance, it might seem cruel that God would "give" someone over to this horrible condition of the mind. But in con-

---

[68] *The Hal Lindsey Report*, Hal Lindsey Website Ministries, August 31, 2010.

PART FOUR: INSANITY BY DESIGN

text we see that God is giving them the thought process they chose. Several places in this passage, we see God giving people the thing they want or the known results of it.

Throughout the latter half of Romans 1, God keeps giving people the reins to their thoughts and lives, either individually, collectively, or both. Romans 1:22 says, "Professing to be wise, they became fools" — cause and effect. Verse 23 says they "changed the glory of the incorruptible God into an image made like corruptible man." Verse 24 says, "Therefore God also gave them up to uncleanness." They wanted corruption, and He let them go where their ugly desires led them.

Verse 25 speaks of people exchanging "the truth of God for the lie." That's intentional. It's done on purpose. The truth of God was embarrassing, difficult, and troublesome. They didn't want it anymore, so they traded it in on a totally different model.

They rejected a clear and sober mind with its knowledge of God as foundation. They did not want God in their understanding. The loss of that most fundamental knowledge warped their perceptions. They chose the reprobate mind when they exchanged the truth of God for a lie. This did not just affect them, but also everyone under their influence.

Without God, they made themselves the center of the universe. It left them without bearing, compass, or plumb line. They became pilots in a fog without reliable instruments. Up became down, and wrong became right. Without reliable orientation, they crashed in on themselves. And because perversion loves company, they spread their poisons everywhere. World-planners tried to steal the world by destroying its moral foundations. This left them with a world hardly worth having.

They exchanged the truth of God for a lie, then suddenly looked around themselves and asked, "What's going on with these kids? Have they lost their minds? We have to do something about the kids!"

The Manchurian Children

The Antichrist may or may not be on the world scene today and, if he is, he will remain hidden until his time has come. That time will be *after* the rapture. What is it that keeps pushing the world into the Antichrist's mold? Simply put, in the Book of Revelation, we find that the Antichrist (the Beast) gets his power from the dragon — Satan, who has been influencing the world for his own agenda since the fall of man took place in the Garden of Eden.

That's the fact that most Christians today appear to forget far too often. There really is a devil! He is not a vapor of evil or the outward expression of the "lizard parts" of our brains. He is an individual. He is not human, but he is a person. He has a story and a personality. He has power, and he is a mighty persuader. I feel for those trying to make sense of history, or of their own lives, if they don't realize that they and humanity have a spiritual enemy. He really exists, and he is not alone.

Through history, most human beings have believed in him in one form or another. But today, he likes to fly under the radar. Few among even his most fervent servants have any understanding of his presence. They serve him, but they have intellectually rejected the idea of him. So, as he entices the world to walk further away from God, people have no idea why everything is falling apart.

But they keep on serving him. They push the drugs and torment the children. Through Hollywood they advocate violence as the answer to everything. The world that rejects God, follows

Satan. If there was any doubt, Jesus called him "the ruler of this world."[69]

The world sacrifices its children on his altars. History tells them that paganism results in bloodshed, in the subjugation of women, in superstition replacing science, in the sexual abuse of others and a thousand other evils. It means pain, death, and an end to human progress.

But their master beckons, and they must follow.

Right now, that master has deliberately set his sights on the sanity of the young. He wants to confuse children, strip them of their families, haunt their every thought, and to make their world a nightmare from which they cannot escape.

In the next few pages, we will look at some of the ways he and his enablers are accomplishing these goals, and ultimately, the purpose it plays regarding the rise of a one world government and the Mark of the Beast.

Love and Hate

When a conservative evangelical talks about LGBTQ issues, we are inevitably accused of "hate speech." It's a reflexive action wired into brains through repetition in schools and the media.

But if someone calls this "hate speech," then that person is the one who doesn't understand. Care compels me to call out a warning to those I see in danger. Caring is not hating. If I see danger ahead — and I do — then to smile and say that the endangered are safe would constitute actual hate speech.

Our society is in danger. Our children are suffering. And

---

[69] John 12:31, 14:30, 16:11.

that suffering will grow intensely more acute in the days and years ahead. I am a preacher of God's word. It is my job to send out His warning as effectively as I can. A warning from God is "love speech."

Troubled Minds… On Purpose

In a Vermont high school, a biological male student joined the girls' volleyball team. The girls asked him not to enter the locker room while they changed clothes. Did this request constitute harassment? The school district opened an investigation. With such investigations, the transgender movement is sweeping away strides made by women in the #MeToo movement.

The girls tried to explain why the presence of a biological male in their dressing room made them uncomfortable. But why should they have to explain? The biological male's presence makes them feel violated. Isn't it enough that they are uncomfortable? The biological male is the one doing something extraordinary — not the girls.

One girl explained, "A male was in our locker room when volleyball girls were trying to get changed. And after I asked him to leave, he didn't, and later looked over at girls with their shirts off. And it made many people uncomfortable and feel violated. And I left as soon as I could in a panic."

Was the bio-male criticized? Did he receive the scorn of others who made women feel violated in the years since #MeToo? No. The girls were roundly criticized and held up to ridicule. The school district investigated them for "harassing someone based on their gender." They also opened an investigation into the event as possible "Hazing, Harassment, and Bullying."

One student said, "Talk about women's rights, we should

have the right to go to the bathroom without a male in our bathroom."

Later, that same Vermont school district suspended a soccer coach without pay because he allegedly "misgendered a transgender student." In other words, he referred to a biological boy using a male pronoun. He used scientifically verifiable and obviously accurate information. But in his case, the district had another motivation. His daughter is one of the girls who pushed back against having the biological male in the girls' locker room while they dressed and undressed.

Many college campuses have their "safe spaces" — places where they feel assured of not hearing an idea that makes them uncomfortable or challenges their prejudices. To me, that sounds like lower education, not higher education. But this is so much more. Surely Americans can agree that a girls' locker room should be a place safe from the prying eyes of biological males. A tiny percent would disagree, and those few are dangerous to the mental health of an entire generation.

MARKING THE MASSES

PART FOUR: INSANITY BY DESIGN

CHAPTER 14

The Rise of Wokeism

Malachi 3:15 says, "So now we call the proud blessed, For those who do wickedness are raised up; They even tempt God and go free." Are the proud blessed? If you are a Christian, think about your answer in light of God's word.

They were once called, "Gay Pride Parades." Now they are just "Pride Parades." No need to leave out transgender individuals or gender fluids or any of the others. Proponents of homosexuality have so taken control of the language that they no longer need to say, "gay pride." "Pride" alone now carries all meanings.

Why the change? Because language becomes a template for the patterns of our thought.

The Power of Language

The power of George Orwell's dystopian novel, *1984*, is not in its foreignness, but in its familiarity. Readers in 1949 recognized it. Despite its outdated view of future technology, *1984* has become even more recognizable today.

In the novel, "Big Brother" government includes a division known as the "thought police." You might wonder how a government could ever police thought. Orwell's solution was profound. "Big Brother" created something called "newspeak." The repressive government changed the meanings of words, creating a new dictionary. With it, the fictional totalitarian government rewired the minds of its citizens. It's a profound theory in fictional writing, but can this work in the real world?

Language profoundly influences thought. We think in concepts, but we also think with words. One of the best ways to change patterns of thought is to change patterns of language. In a 1946 essay, Orwell wrote, "If thought corrupts language, language can also corrupt thought."[70]

Advocates for homosexuality have effectively changed the meaning of the word "pride." Earlier, they changed the meaning of the word "gay." They can also change the popular meaning of symbols. For most people, the US flag once stood for freedom and human dignity. For many today it has become a hated symbol of oppression.

Cartoon rainbows were once relegated to Sunday School flannel boards. To most of today's world, they stand for LGBTQ. (Happily, no cartoon rainbow touches the beauty or magnifi-

---

[70] "Politics and the English Language" by George Orwell, Horizon volume 13, issue 76, April 1946.

cence of a real rainbow arcing across the sky, and still stands for the promise of God.)

Long before Orwell, the Bible talked about the concept of language and its relationship to thought. Isaiah 5:20 says, "Woe to those who call evil good, and good evil; Who put darkness for light, and light for darkness; Who put bitter for sweet, and sweet for bitter!"

Proverbs 17:15 gives another perspective. "He who justifies the wicked, and he who condemns the just, Both of them alike are an abomination to the Lord."

All these things involve words, language. Look at Malachi 2:17. "You have wearied the Lord with your words; Yet you say, 'In what way have we wearied Him?' In that you say, 'Everyone who does evil Is good in the sight of the Lord, And He delights in them,' Or, 'Where is the God of justice?'"

That is a powerful picture of the world in which we live.

The Woke Family

Today, it's becoming commonplace to see parents eager to signal their virtue and to feel good about themselves, take their children to the "Pride Day Parade." Those children will see many things that God says are abominable in His sight.[71] Why would God use such strong language? Because our Creator knows what helps us and what harms us. If anyone is intent on drawing His greatest ire, just harm the children.

Jesus said, "If you cause one of these little ones who trusts in me to fall into sin, it would be better for you to have a large

---

[71] Leviticus 18:22, 20:13, Deuteronomy 12:31, 18:10-12, Provers 3:32, 6:16-19, 17:15,16:5

millstone tied around your neck and be drowned in the depths of the sea. What sorrow awaits the world, because it tempts people to sin. Temptations are inevitable, but what sorrow awaits the person who does the tempting."[72]

According to those rapidly adopting this new language which rewrites morality and accepted social behavior, we keep coming back to a single phrase. Follow the science. If science says morality is self-defined, and our own thoughts and desires create reality – such as one changing themselves from a man to a woman based purely on a mental desire to do so, then I suppose people truly believe they have replaced God with themselves as the genuine authority of creation and law. If one may will themselves into a different being, then there is no limit to what the irrational and debased mind believes it is capable of.

If you can't wrap your mind around this level of insanity, then you're not alone.

Social Insanity

The word "gaslighting" has been increasing in use for the last few years. According to Dictionary.com, the term "originates from a 1938 play… eventually adapted into a film…. The story features a conniving and murderous husband who… makes his wife go crazy…. Part of his efforts include toying with their gas-powered lights so they flicker. He convinces her that she's imagining this, trying to drive her insane."

Today, the word gaslighting refers to "a form of emotional abuse or psychological manipulation involving distorting the truth in order to confuse or create doubt in another person to the

---

[72] Matthew 18:6-7, New Living Translation

PART FOUR: INSANITY BY DESIGN

point they question their sanity or reality."

Convincing someone that the obvious is not real can have ugly ramifications.

It's important to realize that gaslighting is not just an attempt to make a person feel crazy. It is an attempt to drive that person crazy. Gaslighting does this by denying obvious reality. Teaching girls that they are really boys, teaching boys they are really girls, and teaching both that men can become pregnant are all examples of gaslighting on a societal scale.

In a *Star Trek: The Next Generation* episode called "Chain of Command," villainous aliens capture and torture Captain Jean-Luc Picard of the Enterprise. The torture came in many forms. One method was to show the captain four lights, ask him how many lights he saw, and demand the answer, "five." When he refused to say five, his captor inflicted intense physical pain. The idea was to psychologically break him by making him ignore the reality he could see with his own eyes in favor of an obvious lie.

This torture sequence mirrors one in the Orwell novel, *1984*. There, the protagonist must pay a price for writing in his diary, "Freedom is the freedom to say that two plus two make four." His torturer hides his thumb behind his hand and extends four fingers. He asks, "How many fingers am I holding up?" The only "correct" answer is five. That's what *1984*'s "doublethink" requires.

On *Star Trek*, Picard's rescuers finally arrive. As he leaves the torture room, he turns to his tormentor and says, "There! Are! Four! Lights!"

Later he talks about the experience with ship's counselor, Deanna Troi.

Picard: At the end, he gave me a choice — between a life of comfort or more torture. All I had to do was to say that I could see five lights, when in fact there were only four.

Troi: You didn't say it.

Picard: No. No. But I was going to. I would've told him anything. Anything at all. But more than that — I believed that I could see five lights.

When he saw five lights though there were only four, he was experiencing an insanity induced from the outside. And that's what's going on now in schools, on computer screens, on soundstages, etc. all over the world.

In fact, this relentless gaslighting is probably wearing on you as well in some capacity. No one is entirely sheltered from the bombardment of media influence. As we witness increasing social madness and persecution against Christian ideals on the way to the Mark of the Beast, it's critical to actively put on the armor of God each day.

A New Religion

As bad as things are regarding the global cultural shift we are witnessing, there's a more unsettling point to all of this.

The rapid embrace towards the dismantling of traditional families, morality and gender, which I'm going to be referring to as "wokeism", may very well be the foundation of a new global religious system that is prophesied to rise hand-in-hand with the Antichrist's political and financial system during the Tribulation period.

Though most people wouldn't recognize wokeism as a religion, it has all the makings of it. It's not a stretch to see how this superseding worldview could also be defined as one through a biblical lens; no different than other pagan beliefs or practices we've seen throughout human history. Not being openly recognized as such may also increase its deceptiveness as its ideologies are adopted by every peoples, tongues and nations around the world just as we are witnessing. Bible prophecy also describes these global beliefs at the end of days as entirely opposed to Jesus Christ. Again, wokeism fits that bill.

The Final Countdown

If the events described in Revelation are as close as many speculate, then the foundation for these converging end-times events that lead to the fulfillment of prophecy must be unfolding today. This includes the global religious system.

According to the prophetic timeline, logic appears to dictate that the Antichrist doesn't create this global belief, but as with other technologies and political unions, its' already in place by the time he comes to power. As with many politicians today that are leveraging wokeism to implement their radical policies, the Antichrist will do the same.

In fact, as I just mentioned, we know the religious system must be in place by the time the Antichrist comes to power because within a short time, he demands to be worshipped as God — beginning halfway through the seven year Tribulation period. Ironically, the Antichrist and the leaders that give him their authority over the one world government, are said to have despised the world's religious system which is described as the harlot in Revelation. For the Antichrist, the manipulated culture of society becomes nothing more than a means to an end. Once the Beast has reached his goal, the rise to power, the means are done away with.

> *Then he said to me, "The waters which you saw, where the harlot sits, are peoples, multitudes, nations, and tongues. And the ten horns which you saw on the beast, these will hate the harlot, make her desolate and naked, eat her flesh and burn her with fire."*
> — *Revelation 17:15-16*

It's at this time the False Prophet forces the world to shift their worship to the Antichrist. In fact, most of the world will be enthusiastically willing to do so. Those that have already adopted a belief system of lawlessness, encapsulated by wokeism, would easily follow a man of lawlessness — a counterfeit messiah.

Bible prophecy also appears to relate this one world religion to the "strong delusion" that God sends in the last days — that they would believe the lie.[73] What's the lie? That "you will be like God".

> *The coming of the lawless one is according to the working of Satan, with all power, signs, and lying wonders, and with all unrighteous deception among those who perish, because they did not receive the love of the truth, that they might be saved. And for this reason God will send them strong delusion, that they should believe the lie, that they all may be condemned who did not believe the truth but had pleasure in unrighteousness.*
> — *2 Thessalonians 2:9-12*

---

[73] Genesis 3:5

If wokeism is indeed the foundation for the rise of the one world religion, then this could foreshadow just how close we are to the Rapture and to the beginning of the Tribulation.

I previously mentioned how the majority of those that are adopting wokeism are of the Millennial generation and younger (Generation Z and Generation Alpha). As of 2023, this includes those that are 42 years of age and younger. Let me be clear. This group now makes up the majority of the world's population so logic would dictate that wokeism has the potential, if it hasn't already, to become the largest religious belief in the world. At the very least, it's the fastest growing. Everything about this movement appears to be pushing forward the agenda of the elites who are ushering in the one world government.

What About the Rapture?

Most Christians I speak to will claim that because the events of Revelation, which include the rise of the Antichrist and the Mark of the Beast won't occur until after the Rapture, then it's something we don't need to be concerned with or watchful for. Don't make this mistake. We are told to watch and be ready for a reason!

If wokeism leads to the acceptance of the Antichrist and his Mark, then everyone today that is adopting these anti-biblical beliefs are already well on their way to eternal destruction. The dangers of the Mark of the Beast are not only for those living during the Tribulation, but its foundations are already conditioning billions of people all over the world right now!

With the younger generation being the most indoctrinated, this could likely already include your children, or grandchildren. At the very least, someone you know.

PART FIVE

Viral Manipulation

MARKING THE MASSES

PART FIVE: VIRAL MANIPULATION

CHAPTER 15

Could Vaccines Be the Mark of the Beast?

During the height of Covid-19 vaccine mandates, people often asked me if the vaccines were (or contained) the Mark of the Beast. The question may come in part from comments made by men such as Peter Feaman, a Florida lawyer and prominent Republican leader. In May of 2021, he wrote, "Diabolical Michigan Governor Whitmer [sic] wants her citizens to get the Mark of the Beast to participate in society."

I'm sure he's sincere in that belief, but it does not track with the Bible. When people asked me the question, my answer was simple. "Covid vaccines are not the Mark of the Beast, but vaccine mandates are a massive step in that direction." Some who heard me say that became incensed with me. To them it seemed obvious that the vaccines were the Mark, and they couldn't believe that I couldn't see it.

In this chapter, I hope to show why it would be impossible for present Covid vaccines to be or contain the Mark of the Beast. Later, we will look at some of the many ways vaccines and their mandates foreshadow key aspects of the Mark of the Beast. Legally and psychologically, they laid the groundwork for the Mark. They not only put us on the Mark of the Beast highway, but they shoved us a long way down that road.

The Mark of the Beast Needs a Beast

On my March 28, 2022, *Hope For Our Times* livestream, I interviewed Pastor Curt Reed of Harvest Life Christian Fellowship in Las Vegas. We talked about similarities between vaccine mandates and the Mark of the Beast as described in the Bible. And yes, there are disturbing similarities. But Curt pointed out something crucial. "You can't have a Mark of the Beast," he said, "when you don't have a beast."

The Antichrist has not yet come to power. The Bible says Antichrist, also known in scripture as "the lawless one," cannot come to power yet because he is being restrained. 2 Thessalonians 2:7-8 says, "He who now restrains will do so until He is taken out of the way. And then the lawless one will be revealed."

The Restrainer has to be Someone powerful enough to restrain Satan. John F. Walvoord's *Bible Knowledge Commentary* states, "The Holy Spirit of God is the only Person with sufficient (supernatural) power to do this restraining…. How does He do it? Through Christians, whom He indwells and through whom He works in society to hold back the swelling tide of lawless living. How will He be taken out of the way? When the church leaves the earth in the rapture, the Holy Spirit will be taken out of the way in the sense that His unique lawlessness-restraining ministry through God's people will be removed." [74]

The Holy Spirit will be removed at the rapture in a way that mirrors His arrival on the day of Pentecost. We see from many scriptures in both the Old and New Testaments that He was already at work in the world before Pentecost. But Pentecost marked the beginning of the Church. With it, the Holy Spirit took on the job of empowerer and protector of the Church.

Antichrist will not be revealed until the Restrainer (the Holy Spirit working in and through the Church) is removed at the rapture. The Spirit will still be in the world, but with the Church taken into heaven, His role will change. The Church will no longer be on earth doing His will and will no longer need His protection. That is when things on earth go south in a hurry.

Since the Antichrist cannot be revealed until after the rapture, neither can his Mark. Without the beast, there can be no Mark of the Beast.

Keep in mind one other factor. Revelation 13 shows the false prophet being revealed after the Antichrist has come on the scene. And it is the false prophet who will institute the Mark of the Beast system.[75] These events clearly take place after the rapture.

Unrepentant and Unforgiven

According to the Bible, those who receive the Mark will not repent and cannot receive forgiveness. Revelation 14:11 says, "The smoke of their torment ascends forever and ever; and they

---

[74] *Bible Knowledge Commentary/New Testament* Copyright © 1983, 2000 Cook Communications Ministries. All rights reserved.

[75] Revelation 13:11-18

have no rest day or night, who worship the beast and his image, and whoever receives the mark of his name."

There are many possible reasons why no one will repent after receiving the Mark. It may be that the Mark itself will involve technology that takes over a part of the will. They may cease being physically able to change their minds. In any case, at the time they take the Mark, they willfully turn to Satan. The hour of that decision constitutes a last opportunity to turn to Christ.

The phrase, "*Whoever* receives the mark of his name" is clear and definite. The decision to receive the Mark pushes them past the point of no return. The "smoke of their torment ascends forever and ever."

Revelation 20:4 speaks of seeing in heaven those who came to Christ after the rapture. It specifically states that they "had *not* worshiped the beast or his image, and had not received his mark on their foreheads or on their hands."

The Angel's Global Proclamation

> *Then a third angel followed them, saying with a loud voice, "If anyone worships the beast and his image, and receives his mark on his forehead or on his hand, he himself shall also drink of the wine of the wrath of God, which is poured out full strength into the cup of His indignation. He shall be tormented with fire and brimstone in the presence of the holy angels and in the presence of the Lamb. And the smoke of their torment ascends forever and ever; and they have no rest day or night, who worship the beast and his image, and whoever receives the mark of his name."*
>
> *— Revelation 14:9-11*

The angel's words reiterate the eternal character of the choice to receive the Mark. Think about what a big deal this is. I don't know the mechanics of how an angel "flying in the midst of heaven"[76] will speak in a "loud voice," but I do know that all the world will get the news. He tells them that to receive the Mark will result in the eternal damnation of their souls.

Did an angel fly through the heavens making such a proclamation about the vaccines? Then the vaccines are not the Mark of the Beast, nor do they contain it.

Receiving the Mark Involves the Worship of Antichrist and of Satan

Before mentioning the Mark, the angel in Revelation 14:9 says, "If anyone worships the beast and his image...." Revelation 13:3-4 says, "All the world marveled and followed the beast. So they worshiped the dragon who gave authority to the beast; and they worshiped the beast."

<u>Worship is a choice</u>, and they will know the kind of man they are worshiping. He makes no secret of it. Revelation 13:6-7 says, "He opened his mouth in blasphemy against God, to blaspheme His name, His tabernacle, and those who dwell in heaven. It was granted to him to make war with the saints and to overcome them."

He openly speaks against God. He blasphemes God's very name. He has a special hatred for those who have been resurrected or raptured — the people in Christ who are already in heaven.[77] And he makes war on God's people who are on earth.

---

[76] Revelation 14:6

[77] Revelation 13:6

He leaves no doubt about His hatred for God and for all who belong to God.

The false prophet will lead the Mark of the Beast program. One of his purposes will be to make every person on earth worship the Antichrist. Revelation 13:11-18 makes clear that the Mark of the Beast system is not just about the economics of buying and selling. It is also about the worship of a man — Antichrist.

"And he [the false prophet]... causes the earth and those who dwell in it to worship the first beast."[78]

Receiving a Covid vaccine does not turn people into worshipers of Satan.

Penalties Will Be More Extreme

Vaccine mandates cost people their jobs and careers. They have caused social and economic ruin for countless men and women. They caused the heartbreak of foreclosure and bankruptcy. But no one mandated the beheading of people refusing the vaccines.

Revelation 20:4 says, "Then I saw the souls of those who had been beheaded for their witness to Jesus and for the word of God, who had not worshiped the beast or his image, and had not received his mark on their foreheads or on their hands."

Refusal to receive the Mark will take away a person's ability to buy and sell. The mandates cost people their jobs, but they didn't entirely take away their ability to buy or sell. To buy something may have meant dipping into savings, but there was no law against the unvaccinated buying groceries at a local store

---

[78] Revelation 13:12

or purchasing electronics over the internet. Those without the Mark will be excluded from all commerce.

Punishments for the unmarked will not stop there. Refusing the mark will become a capital offense. The unmarked will face beheading. Vaccine mandates were bad, but not that bad.

A Couple of Other Differences…

They inject Covid vaccines into the shoulder. The Mark of the Beast will be placed either on the right hand or the forehead.

Remember that Satan and his men use deception in getting people to take the Mark, but it won't be the simple trickery of slipping it into medicine. Receiving the Mark will be an eternal choice, not a casual trip to the Walmart® pharmacy.

Finally, one of the discouraging aspects of Covid vaccines has been their ineffectiveness over time. In a matter of months (maybe less) they lose whatever effectiveness they may have had at the beginning. The Mark of the Beast will be a one-and-done event. No need for a booster.

MARKING THE MASSES

PART FIVE: VIRAL MANIPULATION

CHAPTER 16

What Vaccine Mandates Teach Us

The Covid vaccine is not the Mark of the Beast, but the coercion surrounding vaccine mandates looks eerily familiar to those who have studied Bible prophecy. Methods used to enforce the mandates mirror those that the Antichrist and false prophet will use to enforce the Mark of the Beast. Primarily, they dangled the sword of economic ruin over the heads of the uncompliant.

Beware of Government Empowering Itself

The government fired longtime employees who refused the shot. They encouraged businesses to fire any employee who did not receive a vaccination. They tried to push through an OSHA plan forcing businesses with 100 or more employees to fire workers who did not get the vaccine and could not or would not submit to weekly tests. In many cases, the employees had to pay for the expensive tests, an onerous burden on low-income workers. City and county governments forced firefighters and police to get shots or face retribution. A high number of medical personnel lost jobs because they refused the shot.

First responders and medical personnel were the toast of the nation during the worst of the pandemic. We called them heroes. They put themselves at risk for the wellbeing of others. Then, a few months later, they found themselves being fired for noncompliance.

The courts overruled or scaled back many of the mandates. But the point is, government freely instituted onerous and obviously unconstitutional rules. Worse, they successfully convinced the media and a high percentage of the public to support those rules.

Governments of the world over used the possibility of financial ruin as a bludgeon against citizens who had done nothing wrong. They used social pressure, career limitations, travel restrictions, and educational constraints along with limits on the ability to buy and sell. They used a carrot and stick approach, making it financially and socially profitable to comply while being disastrous to your way of life if you don't.

A vaccine, when forced on an individual, becomes a supreme violation that takes away freedom of choice regarding your health. I would equate it to governments and corporations forcing individuals to gamble with their very lives. If there is a risk, then there should be a choice, but the powers that be no longer see you as an individual nor do they care about your freedom. To me, this is reminiscent of the Pharaohs and Caesars of the ancient world that placed themselves up as gods among men. Their lives have meaning while yours does not.

PART FIVE: VIRAL MANIPULATION

The Rallying Cry of the Tyrant

Clinton Administration official and former Chicago mayor, Rahm Emanuel, famously said, "Never let a serious crisis go to waste. And what I mean by that it's an opportunity to do things you think you could not do before."

It is not necessarily immoral to use circumstances as a means of pushing policies you believe will help. However, creating or exaggerating a crisis for that purpose is immoral. James Madison is reputed to have said, "Crisis is the rallying cry of the tyrant."

And with Covid, that's what happened. The people pushing a globalist, antichristian agenda, exaggerated Covid. They created chaos so that they could use their ideas and programs to "fix it." They assigned blame for Covid's spread on groups they considered undesirable — like Bible-believing Christians. Then they tried to shut them up and shut them down.

Financial Life or Death

In times of crisis, when people are desperate, they become especially pliable to the will of their leaders. When the mob gets scared, they do whatever they think will make them safe. And few things are as scary as economic destruction.

In 2022, economists in Venezuela were excited by the fact that the inflation rate there had gotten all the way down to 222%. A look at their recent history explains their pleasure in such horrible numbers. In 2018, the Venezuelan inflation rate soared far above 100,000%. Some published reports set it at one million percent. Imagine what that does to the average household, or to the person who saved all her life so she could have a comfortable old age. 100,000% inflation obliterated lifetimes of savings in a matter of days.

That level of economic upheaval means homelessness and starvation for previously middle-class citizens. With a threat like that hanging over their heads, the world's nations would suddenly be willing to do almost anything.

The strains of Covid we have seen so far kill only a tiny percentage of those infected. Yet doctors and media made it seem so dire that people willingly gave up their dearest rights — things like freedom of religion, freedom of speech, and freedom of assembly. Imagine what the fear of mass starvation would do? That's how Antichrist will come to power without firing a shot. Fear will conquer the world for him.

Eyes Everywhere

During the Covid crisis, people were encouraged to turn in noncompliant neighbors. Teachers instructed their students to tell authorities if their parents broke the Covid rules. Authorities enlisted businesses. Government at all levels enforced mandates, masks, and social distancing.

The Antichrist's government will be the most oppressive in history, and it will work (though only briefly) with the help of citizen spies.

'It Was About Compliance'

An October 2022 article in the Heritage Foundation's media arm, *The Daily Signal*, puts this in a unique perspective. "A New York judge ordered Monday that Department of Sanitation employees terminated for refusing to get vaccinated be reinstated to their full employment status, writing that the vaccination mandate for city employees was 'not just about safety and public health; it was about compliance.'

"Judge Ralph J. Porzio wrote in his ruling that if the vaccine mandate was about 'safety and public health, unvaccinated workers would have been placed on leave the moment the order was issued.'

"'If it was about safety and public health, the Health Commissioner would have issued city-wide mandates for vaccination for all residents,' he continued. 'In a City with a nearly 80% vaccination rate, we shouldn't be penalizing the people who showed up to work, at great risk to themselves and their families, while we were locked down.'"[79]

The judge's phrase should be chilling to us all. "It was about compliance." I think that means it was about control, obedience, the removal of power from individuals, and the investing of power in the state... just like the Mark of the Beast.

This isn't an isolated event of ideals regarding your worth and freedom as an individual either. In November of 2022, the G20 Summit met and issued a joint declaration promoting a global health passport with a global digital health network that will provide proof of vaccinations for international travel. It is likely only a matter of time when some form of this comes about but imagine this isn't strictly for international travelers, but for those flying from state to state. Only those who comply may continue with their lives as they were. For everyone else, that's another story.

---

[79] "New York Supreme Court Reinstates Unvaccinated Employees With Backpay: 'It Was About Compliance'" by Mary Margaret Olohan, *The Daily Signal*, October 25, 2022

Arrests

Earlier, in April of 2020, a church in Mississippi hosted a drive-in church service. People stayed in their cars. Parishioners did not have to roll their windows down to hear because the church used a radio frequency that could be picked up on car radios. They held the meeting outside where catching Covid is almost impossible. They were not only socially distanced but cocooned within their own cars.

They had no contact with other people... until the police showed up and started issuing $500 tickets. Then the windows went down, and the doors opened. In some cases, a husband and wife within the same car, each received a $500 ticket. The issue was not about staying safe from Covid. This church went above and beyond in their attempt to abide by safe practices. The town was trying to abide by intentionally vague federal guidance. For some in the federal bureaucracy, the real issue was about setting a precedent for government hobbling churches.

Across the world, governments placed onerous restrictions on movement and transportation, effectively imprisoning people in small communities or in their homes. Various nations gave health officials the power to put their citizens under house arrest — having committed no crime and having received no due process. As I write this, many in China remain under house arrest in what will almost certainly be a futile attempt to stop yet another Covid variant.

These are foretastes of the world of Antichrist and his Mark.

PART FIVE: VIRAL MANIPULATION

The Money Bomb

Covid-19 vaccine mandates wrecked careers. People spent decades working hard to enter professions and then advance in them. Mandates cut many of them off at the knees. Others held jobs that barely paid the bills. For them, mandates meant comply or go on the government dole. Police officers, firefighters, doctors, nurses, soldiers, and teachers — were fired, often without a hearing.

Governments and corporations intimidated employees, coercing them into taking a vaccine those employees believed to be harmful. The alternative was stop being able to take care of their families. Money for survival is an overwhelming motivator — almost irresistible. With Covid as an excuse, left-wing government and business leaders used the power of money against the people. We have an inherent need for the dignity of work and to provide for family. The threat to cut off money is not just a threat against adults, but against their kids.

In the future, people who refuse Antichrist's Mark will cease to receive a paycheck — just like many of those who refused Covid vaccines. But refusing the Mark will be worse. The unmarked will not be able to receive payments or make payments. Even if they have money saved, without the Mark they will not be able to buy anything with that money.

Covid vaccine mandates gave us a terrible taste of this horrible future.

MARKING THE MASSES

PART FIVE: VIRAL MANIPULATION

CHAPTER 17

Crushing Human Rights

One of the scarier things about vaccine mandates was the lack of knowledge of what the vaccines will do to human bodies over time. It seems reasonable to ask if a vaccine developed in a few months has been fully evaluated for long-term side effects. Is that even possible?

If you watch television, you see lawyers advertising for people to join class action lawsuits against drug manufacturers. The FDA has removed drugs from the market as unsafe, including drugs that went through nearly a decade of testing. Parents see this, and they think about the safety of their children. Hopefully, their children have long lives ahead of them, decades during which ill effects from the vaccine could manifest themselves.

Child Abuse?

We also see pharmaceutical companies' own ads. They spend

as much time with disclaimers telling the awful side effects as they do touting the products. "Nausea, vomiting, permanent hearing loss, boils, and amputations. Do not take this product if you are allergic to it. <u>Be sure to call your doctor in case of death.</u>"

Those are the parts of the ads insisted on by the lawyers. That's not necessary when talking about Covid vaccines because governments gave immunity to vaccine-makers before they even created any products. Findlaw.com writes, "To encourage the development and use of new vaccines, including the COVID-19 vaccine, the federal government granted drugmakers substantial immunity from personal injury and product liability lawsuits involving vaccines."

Drug stores and medical aids gave vaccines to a massive number of people who experienced a wide variety of side effects. The media kept that part of the news as quiet as possible.

I'm not saying people should avoid giving their children Covid vaccines. That is a personal, medical decision, and I'm not a doctor. I am saying that reasonable people can differ on whether to take the vaccine. I'm saying that parents who were resistant to giving their children a Covid vaccine had thoughtful arguments on their side. They should not have been labeled "child abusers."

But they were.

Human Rights Give Way to Government Power

Americans who stopped to consider what was happening, could hardly believe it. It was like watching the Constitution of the United States slipping away into a shredding machine.

The first ten amendments to the US Constitution, known as the Bill of Rights, have become key parts of the foundation of our democracy. The First Amendment protects the freedoms of religion, speech, and assembly. Traditionally, Americans viewed this amendment as the most sacred of secular laws because it codifies divinely given rights. Many countries, including China, have similar rules on paper, but they don't always mean much. In the United States, they had always been primary... until Covid.

Look what the government did to those laws during Covid.

- Freedom of religion? They shut down houses of worship. They limited the number of participants and even prohibited Christians from singing the hallowed songs of our faith.

- Freedom of speech? By openly pressuring Silicon Valley social media companies, the government succeeded in shutting down naysayers. If you said the wrong thing — if you just questioned vaccine orthodoxy — you could be fired, lose a government contract, or be knocked off an online media platform. (I know the last one from multiple firsthand experiences.)

- Freedom of assembly? Officials gave massive fines to pastors and even arrested some for allowing their congregations to assemble for church on Sunday mornings... *in America!*

Oceans of Propaganda

During the height of Covid mandates, the world's media turned themselves into propaganda machines. Social media platforms treated good people like terrorists for simply raising questions about the legality of vaccine mandates or the efficacy and safety of the vaccines themselves. Major newspapers, most TV news outlets, and almost every other mainstream news organization stopped the practice of journalism and joined one side of the debate.

Straight journalists — as opposed to opinion writers — give both sides of major debates. But with Covid, reporters considered actual journalism morally wrong. They did their best to make the unruly masses more compliant with government edicts. They painted adversaries of the status quo as enemies whose opinions amounted to crimes against humanity.

That presents another lesson about the world of Antichrist and his Mark. The media will make people feel like the Mark of the Beast is this glorious new thing. Only losers, they will say, ever refuse it. They will paint the "losers" as racists who hate the environment and want children to die young. If anyone in media tries to tell the other side, he or she will be silenced.

We are quickly losing news sources that at least try to be objective. This is an incalculable loss to human civilization. Choosing advocacy over objectivity robs citizens of trustworthy sources of information. That's because an advocate only looks for the facts that back up her point of view. A real journalist reports facts, as much as possible holding her opinion to herself. Her report will allow people on the various sides of the issue to express the opposing positions. Government of the people, by the people, for the people *requires* some sources of unfiltered data.

The truth is still out there, of course, but it is so shrouded in lies and hate that it can be tough to see. Even if seen, it has often been beaten beyond recognition. In the days of Antichrist and the Mark, getting the truth to the people will require fiery witnesses and an angel calling out from the heavens.

PART FIVE: VIRAL MANIPULATION

'These Aren't the Droids You're Looking For'

Never mind what you see, feel, and experience. Take our word for it. Everything is great. There's nothing to see here. Move along.

Most Americans remember Obi-Wan Kenobi's Jedi mind trick in the original Star Wars movie. Kenobi is a "Jedi Master" — a sort of warrior-priest of the Jedi religion. The religion centers around an entity known as "The Force." Kenobi explains, "The Force is what gives a Jedi his power. It's an energy field created by all living things. It surrounds us and penetrates us. It binds the galaxy together."

The film's main protagonist, Luke Skywalker, travels through a city with Kenobi and two "droids" — short for android. In Star Wars, droids are robots with varying degrees of artificial intelligence. With the galactic empire searching for these particular droids, Kenobi and friends reach a checkpoint.

Stormtrooper to Skywalker: "Let me see your identification."
Kenobi: "You don't need to see his identification."
Stormtrooper: "We don't need to see his identification."
Kenobi: "These aren't the droids you're looking for."
Stormtrooper: "These aren't the droids we're looking for."
Kenobi: "He can go about his business."
Stormtrooper (a voice of authority): "You can go about your business."

Later, Luke says, "I don't understand how we got by those troops. I thought we were dead."

To this, Obi-Wan replies, "The Force can have a strong influence on the weak-minded."

Many readers could have recited these lines verbatim, but do they apply here? Global elites use the forces of propaganda, trust of authority figures, and outright deception to influence everyone they can.

A CNBC article from October of 2022 illustrates the Kenobi-style technique. "If you already got your omicron-specific Covid booster, you might have experienced some side effects. Maybe even ones that were more intense than your previous shot. But there's no need to worry: Experts and new data say the new shots appear to work — regardless of whether you experience moderate, mild or no side effects at all."[80]

Pay no attention to what you feel, or to what your friends and family who receive the new version of the vaccine tell you about their experience. Everything is hunky-dory. Don't worry about the intense headaches, fever, rashes, swollen glands, upset stomachs, achy joints, and fatigue. Even though the first humans ever to receive these new vaccine versions started getting them only a month or so earlier, "experts" say you have nothing to worry about.

It is an amazing thing when a major news outlet is willing to go that far in touting the party line. Ignore the symptoms, no matter how bad they get. Experts have waved their hands and spoken. These aren't the health concerns you should be looking for.

That is a powerful picture of how most of the world will fall under the sway of Antichrist and his Mark. They will use other

---

[80] "Omicron-specific Covid boosters appear to work well, new data says—regardless of the side effects you experience" by Annika Kim Constantino, CNBC, October 15, 2022.

techniques as well, up to and including the threat of death. But big threats only work if the majority goes along. And they will go along through the powerful application of propaganda.

Fake News and Free Speech

In April of 2022, Germany passed a law against "fake news." Wenzel Michalski, the German director of Human Rights Watch, said of the law, "It is vague, overbroad, and turns private companies into overzealous censors to avoid steep fines, leaving users with no judicial oversight or right to appeal."

Russia has a law that can fine people the equivalent of 6,000 US dollars for saying anything online that shows "blatant disrespect" for the government. "Blatant disrespect" is in the eye of the beholder. It can include anything the officials want it to include. It is purposely vague to make the individual increasingly vulnerable to an ever more powerful governmental elite.

The European Union recently passed "the Digital Services Act" or "DSA." In April of 2022, the European Commission said, "The DSA sets out an unprecedented new standard for the accountability of online platforms regarding illegal and harmful content."

The DSA doesn't just target illegal content. It bars "harmful content" and it allows technocrats to arbitrarily decide what qualifies as "harmful." The DSA affects companies like Alphabet (including Google and YouTube), Meta (including Facebook, Instagram, and WhatsApp), Twitter, Microsoft, and even Amazon — companies whose products touch all our lives.

The Commission's press release quoted one of the Commissioners, Thierry Breton. He said the DSA "entrusts the Commission with supervising very large platforms." That makes it clear.

The European Commission now sees itself as the supervisor of these major communications platforms. They will police the algorithms Google uses when giving you search results.

One Commissioner promised that the DSA will "prevent dangerous disinformation from going viral."[81] That's an astonishing thing to say. And it does not just affect Europe. The algorithms they plan to police are used everywhere.

Such laws are at least partially a response to what they call "Covid misinformation." Covid became the excuse to write the laws and put the systems in place that will undergird the Mark of the Beast.

The DHS's 'Disinformation Governance Board'

In April of 2022, the US Department of Homeland Security (DHS) announced that it was forming something with the Orwellian-sounding title, "the Disinformation Governance Board" or "DGB."

The Department of Homeland Security was founded in order "to develop and coordinate the implementation of a comprehensive national strategy to secure the United States from terrorist threats or attacks."[82] DHS is a law enforcement agency that coordinates the CIA, FBI, Customs and Border Patrol, Coast Guard, and the Secret Service among many others in the fight against terrorism. To put the Disinformation Governance Board within DHS gives the Board teeth. Its edicts would be

---

[81] Margrethe Vestager quoted in the European Commission press release

[82] From the October 2001 Executive Order Establishing the Office of Homeland Security.

backed up by the agencies with guns.

A month after they announced it, the White House put DGB on "pause." The pause follows a major public backlash against the idea of the government supervising free speech and a free press. The thing had been blatantly unconstitutional from the beginning. *[handwritten: GOVERMENT PROPAGANDA CHANNEL]*

After the pause, NPR ran a story that showed up on search engines with the title, "How DHS's disinformation board fell victim to misinformation." Written by tech correspondent, Shannon Bond, NPR presented it as a straight news story. They did not label it an opinion piece.

NPR called the woman who was to head the Disinformation Governance Board, Nina Jankowicz, "A well-regarded authority in online disinformation." The story said that Jankowicz "came under relentless and sometimes vicious attack from right-wing media.... Conservatives seized on her tweets and past public statements as evidence of her partisan bias."

In this era of human rage, I'm sure horrible things were said to and about Ms. Jankowicz. But to question her personal bias was not horrible, and it was not "disinformation." Public officials should be neither surprised nor offended by scrutiny. She was taking on a public role unlike anything in US history. Journalists must examine people who take positions of power in our government.

In this case, what the "conservative media" said was true. She is an extreme partisan. That is not a political criticism, but a fact. *Daily Signal* contributor, Jarrett Stepman, wrote, "She cast doubt on the veracity of the Hunter Biden laptop story, which was confirmed to be true. She dismissed the idea that COVID-19 originated in a lab in Wuhan, China, as nothing more than a way to give then-President Donald Trump a scapegoat for the pandemic. Clearly, there's a good reason to believe that story, even if China makes finding the truth difficult, if not impossible.

"In addition, Jankowicz backed since-debunked claims that Trump was connected to a Kremlin-backed bank. What's more, she has an extensive public record of seeing any story that counters left-wing narratives or makes Democrats in general look bad as examples of disinformation."[83]

In other words, she is exactly what the technology reporter for NPR said she was not. Jankowicz resigned after the White House put the program on pause. But the pause was not the victory many constitutionalists thought it was. We need to remember how these things work. A common strategy of government activists is to push an extreme agenda — often so extreme they know it cannot stand. Then they pull back, but not all the way. It looked like they were pushed back, but in practical terms, they moved society in the direction they wanted it to go. They gained ground.

That happened here. The administration paused DGB. It did not end it. White House Press Secretary, Karine Jean-Pierre, said their work "to address disinformation that threatens the security of our country is critical, and that will indeed continue." In other words, their attempts to pressure and bully businesses into censoring free speech will continue, and even be enhanced.

Stepman wrote, "The Biden administration seemingly took George Orwell's book *1984* as a guide, rather than as a warning."[84]

---

[83] "Now-Abandoned Disinformation Board Was Insult to Free Society" by Jarrett Stepman, *The Daily Signal*, May 18, 2022

[84] Ibid.

PART FIVE: VIRAL MANIPULATION

Real Motives

Notice how elites used the Covid tyrannies to attack what they already hated. Back in 2016, the US Civil Rights Commission issued a report on religious freedom and non-discrimination. After three years in preparation, the report turned out to be an attack on the First Amendment.

Martin Castro, then the chairman of the US Civil Rights Commission, said, "The phrases 'religious liberty' and 'religious freedom' will stand for nothing except hypocrisy so long as they remain code words for discrimination, intolerance, racism, sexism, homophobia, Islamophobia, Christian supremacy or any form of intolerance."

He contends that "religious liberty" and "religious freedom" are "code words" for the things he most detests in his fellow human beings. He's wrong, of course. Religious liberty means freedom of worship for the Muslim as well as the Christian, the homosexual as well as the heterosexual, and for all races.

Roger Severino of the Ethics and Public Policy Center called the Commission's report an "attempt to discredit sincere religious believers as being motivated by hate instead of faith and the implied recommendation that religious groups should change their beliefs on sexual morality to conform with liberal norms for the good of the country. I would expect to see such a slanted and anti-religious report come out of China or France perhaps, but am disappointed to see it come from the U.S. Commission on Civil Rights."

The Mark of the Beast system will be far worse, but with eerie similarities. When you get on I90 East in Seattle, you are still a continent away from Boston. You're not in Boston yet, but you are on the road that takes you there.

I began this book with a story my dad told me about a group of men that later had profound influence on advances in technology and science with an agenda to control the world. Discoveries and advances to this day are foundations to the ever closer development of the Beast system. Over the last 60 years, their goals never changed as their influence expanded to consume government leaders, corporate executives, professors and humanists. Those that stood in the back yard at that party overlooking the Hollywood Hills may have assumed the world would be their oyster, but the truth is that they have been pawns for the Devil. It's his system, not theirs, that they have been building all along.

Few genuine followers of Christ would deny we're on the very path to the Mark of the Beast right now. We may not be there quite yet, but we have a solid idea of what it will be like.

PART SIX

Beast World

MARKING THE MASSES

PART SIX: BEAST WORLD

CHAPTER 18

The Beast System

What Does "666" Mean?

Revelation 13:18 says, "Here is wisdom. Let him who has understanding calculate the number of the beast, for it is the number of a man: His number is 666."

The beast's name will in some way correlate to the number 666. In the Bible, six relates to man while seven relates to God. Seven means completeness and perfection. Six means incomplete and imperfect. Romans 3:23 tells us, "All have sinned and fall short of the glory of God." That is the human condition — "short of the glory of God" — a six and not a seven.

Antichrist will demand worship, but he will not be worthy of worship. His is the number of a man and not of God. In the *Jewish New Testament Commentary*, David H. Stern wrote, "Triple repetition symbolizes absolute ultimacy (as in Isaiah 6:3, 'Holy, holy, holy is Adonai of Hosts').... 666 means that the beast in every respect falls short of perfection and is therefore absolutely and ultimately imperfect and evil."[85]

The Bible goes on to say, "Let him who has understanding calculate the number of the beast."[86]

In both the Greek and Hebrew alphabets, letters correspond to numbers. So, "the number of the beast" may be as simple as adding up the numbers associated with the letters in his name. But beware of this. People trying to use this method to ID the Antichrist have caused great confusion and made many false accusations.

In prophecy as in life, proximity tends to increase clarity. As we draw closer in time to prophetic events, we see them better. At this point, we may not yet understand how to "calculate the number of the beast" because we don't need to know. People who come to Christ after the rapture will need to know how to calculate the beast's number. I am convinced that when they need it, God in His mercy will grant them that understanding.

Why the Hand or Forehead?

Revelation 13:16 says, "He causes all… to receive a mark on their right hand or on their foreheads." Why?

The face is the world's most common bio-identifier. We use it on passports and drivers' licenses. Friends and family use it to recognize one another. The face as an identifier makes it diffi-

---

[85] *Jewish New Testament Commentary* by David H. Stern, Copyright © 1992.

[86] Revelation 13:18

cult for movie stars to eat at restaurants in peace. Our faces identify us. Phones and other computers also use facial recognition. So, as a place for the mark, the forehead makes perfect sense.

The forehead is also near another bio-identifier — one that is almost infallible — the human retina. Exhaled breath from two other facial features, the nose and mouth, is as unique to each person as a fingerprint, partly because everyone's gut flora is different. And don't forget that the most common way to take a DNA sample is with a mouth swab.

The second most common bio-identifier is the fingerprint, along with palm and thumb prints. That fits the other location for the Mark of the Beast — the hand.

To us, those locations seem obvious. But the Book of Revelation was written 1900 years ago. Who then knew anything about machines that would someday recognize faces, process retina scans, or identify someone based on his fingerprint or gut flora?

What Will the Physical Mark Be?

The Bible is not specific on this question. It gives us intriguing clues, but it also leaves the door open to many possibilities.

People have long suspected that the Mark would consist of a tattoo — perhaps of the actual number 666. Others imagine something like a barcode or QR code using an easily recognized general pattern that includes 666, but somehow individualized. A scanner might read the code, then connect to your cloud account at Big Brother headquarters. This would be simple and inexpensive, but perhaps too easily circumvented.

With dogs, we use microchips. A chip could simultaneously track a person's location, financial data, medical history, present vital signs, social credit score, and many other things about the individual. The chip itself would not need to be large or powerful because it would connect to the cloud.

Whatever it is, we can be sure the Mark will include something physical. It won't be as simple as putting a person's name on a list. It will do more than just show someone as a member in good standing of the global economy. It will mark them as a person with total allegiance to the Antichrist — not just a follower, but a worshiper.

Will the Mark Be Visible?

Since the Bible calls it a "mark," we know it will be seen. But seen by whom — or what? There are marks the human eye cannot see. But they allow humans to open locked doors or start their cars. Even when your smartphone rests in your pocket or purse, safely hidden from human eyes, it stays "visible" to a vast global network of computers. A chip would not mark the outer body, but it would mark a person electronically. Also, we might be talking about a combination of an outer mark and inner device.

Many of those illegally entering the United States are given a "dumbed-down" smartphone. This allows the government to track them and communicate with them. "Dumbed-down" means the users cannot access all the phone's capabilities. But they are still there and can easily be turned on. All over the world, governments and charitable organizations give smartphones to the poor at little or no cost. Proponents say that phones are essential. Some even call them a "human right."

Smartphones are wonderful tools and might help people escape poverty. But these devices also allow governments to track people. This is one of the ways that the world's governments and elites are building the infrastructure of the Mark of the Beast system. And they're building it right now.

An Implanted Chip?

In June of 2021, researchers announced that they had built the world's smallest implantable chip. Called "motes," these chips have a volume of less than one cubic millimeter. You need a microscope just to see one. They are easily injectable. But they are not the Mark of the Beast. They have severely limited capabilities. They do not track the user and can only communicate outside the body with the use of an ultrasound machine.

Yet the potential is breathtaking. *Popular Mechanics* reported, "Scientists at Columbia University… hope that one day, the chips can monitor everything from blood pressure, to glucose, to respiration."[87]

This is just one of many injectable chips under development. Some can replace keycards. Others monitor various medical conditions. Make a chip small enough to be injected, but a little larger than a mote, and it can become immensely more powerful. They will not need to hold substantial amounts of information but will function as a key to unlocking the practically unlimited data held in "the cloud." It will work in conjunction with nearby smart devices like phones, TVs, cars, and watches.

Governments and industry are spending vast sums on the development of implantable chips. Most of that development is top secret, but we know it will be revolutionary, and it is coming soon.

---

[87] "Yes, Scientists Built the World's Smallest Implantable Chip. But Don't Freak Out," by Courtney Linder, Popular Mechanics, June 11, 2021.

In or On?

Revelation 13:16 says, "He causes all... to receive a mark on their right hand or on their foreheads." The King James Version says, "in their right hand, or in their foreheads." Most other versions say "on" or "upon."

The Greek word used here is "epi." In English, we usually translate it as "on." The word "epidermis" refers to the outer layer of skin. "Epidemic" combines the Greek word epi with "demos" meaning people. It means "on the people."

But it can also mean "in" or "among" the people. In Greek, "epi" is used in a variety of ways. There are 890 instances of it in the New Testament. English versions of the Bible most often translate it "on," but also translate it as "in" or "into."

The important thing is that in God's eyes, they are marked. Whether it rests on the outer part of the skin or underneath it, they are marked and marked forever.

PART SIX: BEAST WORLD

CHAPTER 19

Brave New Possibilities

The Mark's proponents will convince people to see government access to all their data as not only convenient, but essential.

Imagine a severe car wreck. A woman lies unconscious. Paramedics rush to her aid. They know precisely where to find her. While still en route, they examine her medical history. They look at a list of her present medications and any medications to which she has an allergy. A chip in her body might transmit all her vital signs, allowing them to evaluate her current condition before they arrive. That's more than convenient. It could be lifesaving.

Even an individualized tattoo can allow a computer to find potentially lifesaving information. Think of someone going to a small, locally owned pharmacy half a world away from home. He buys an over-the-counter medication. The Mark system could crosscheck the new medication with every drug or supplement previously purchased by that individual. It could also check the new medicine against the patient's known medical conditions. If the Mark involves a computer chip, it could even watch for side-effects.

The Brain-Computer Interface

Nothing we have yet seen will equal what's coming and what's possible.

Whatever you may think of him, Elon Musk has been a master at taking ideas that were theoretically possible, then making them real. With Tesla and SpaceX, he didn't invent the future. The inventions were mostly already there. Instead, he built the future. But none of them — not Tesla, The Boring Company, Hyperloop, not even SpaceX with Starlink — has the world-changing potential of something called Neuralink.

The goal is to create a data link between the human brain and digital devices. Musk described it as an "electrode to neuron interface at a micro level." He also called it, "a chip and a bunch of tiny wires" that will be "implanted in your skull."[88]

Founded in 2016, the company believes their devices will one day cure or mitigate dementia, spinal cord injuries, deafness, and blindness. At a news conference in 2020, Musk described one prototype as "a Fitbit in your skull."

By 2021, the company gave a demonstration showing a Macaque monkey playing the video game Pong — not using his hands, but his thoughts.

---

[88] "Elon Musk: Humans must merge with machines" by Mike Allen and Jim VandeHei, *Axios*, November 26, 2018.

PART SIX: BEAST WORLD

Knowledge Rentals

Elon Musk has often stated his concern that Artificial Intelligence endangers the human species. He has called it "the scariest problem" and a "fundamental existential risk for human civilization."[89] In 2014, he said, "I like to just keep an eye on what's going on with artificial intelligence.... There have been movies about this, you know, like '[The] Terminator.' There are some scary outcomes."[90]

He warns that, "As the algorithms and the hardware improve, that digital intelligence will exceed biological intelligence by a substantial margin."[91] But he has an answer. Combine human intelligence with AI. "The long-term aspiration with Neuralink," Musk said, "would be to achieve a symbiosis with artificial intelligence."

Now imagine that your brain is hardwired to this device. Long term, the advantages are stunning. When you buy a book, you don't download something to your computer, but to a storage device connected you your AI-brain interface. If you rent the book, you lose the knowledge in a few days. Purchase a book, and its knowledge becomes yours permanently, allowing you to access it whenever you want.

Theatrical presentations could be more real than life. You could mentally control devices in your home or take a look at

---

[89] "Elon Musk's biggest worry" by Konstantin Kakaes, *Politico*, April 26, 2022.

[90] "Elon Musk warned of a 'Terminator'-like AI apocalypse — now he's building a Tesla robot" by Brandon Gomez, *CNBC*, August 24, 2021.

[91] "Elon Musk: Humans must merge with machines" by Mike Allen and Jim VandeHei, *Axios*, November 26, 2018.

your children from across the world. With an effective AI-brain interface, your mind would expand from the limits of your brain into worlds of cyberspace and all the things put there by billions of other people.

Scary Outcomes

<u>A brain that can be wired can also be controlled.</u> Buy a new car today and its computer system may include a feature called over-the-air updates. That means that the manufacturer can send out updates to the car's software. It might make the engine run better, tweak the transmission and suspension for "sport mode," add a new feature to the user interface, fix a security breach, etc.

Drugs might no longer be needed to make someone feel good. Coffee would be needed only for the flavor, aroma, and warmth — not for a caffeine fix or to get you going in the mornings.

Psychiatry would have wondrous tools available to it — but the need for it would fall dramatically. The chip might monitor and adjust such brain chemicals as dopamine. Imagine the promise of an anxiety free, always enthusiastic outlook.

It might monitor which parts of the brain are doing the most work. If it gets the impression that there could be something wrong, it would notify authorities for a closer look. The chip would monitor words, again looking for areas where the individual might be going off the rails.

"Off the rails" might include the possibility of committing a crime or causing self-harm. It might also include "harmful attitudes" expressed in conversations, types of entertainment consumed, etc. With AI monitoring such things, officials could mitigate mass shooter incidents. They might also end votes for the "wrong kind of political candidates."

The chip might help people with their psychological treatments, exercise routines, and even religious practices like meditation or prayer.

A brain directly or indirectly connected to the world wide web would also have over-the-air updates, including how you should feel about a new government edict, etc. Behavior modification might be a major feature. It could turn into a "Stepford" world in no time at all.

Even if the Mark of the Beast turns out to be an implanted chip, I don't believe it will feature the abilities I just described. While I'm convinced that such technology is possible, it seems too far away. The Bible's description of the Mark doesn't require such abilities, and things are moving fast. I don't think humanity will have time to develop these technologies before the Mark is implemented.

However, it is possible that the Mark could have a rudimentary computer-brain interface and promise to be the platform on which more sophisticated versions can be added.

MARKING THE MASSES

PART SIX: BEAST WORLD

CHAPTER 20

The Beast's Reign

How Do We Know Antichrist's Government Will be Totalitarian?

Merriam-webster.com defines "totalitarian" in this way. A) "Of or relating to centralized control by an autocratic leader or hierarchy." B) "Of or relating to a political regime based on subordination of the individual to the state and strict control of all aspects of the life and productive capacity of the nation especially by coercive measures (such as censorship and terrorism)."

This gives a powerful picture of the Soviet Union, Nazi Germany, and similar states. But those nations did not have the technology available today. They could not track every citizen's every move. They could not look through walls. They didn't have access to live images from millions of cameras or sounds from millions of microphones. They did not have a global network connecting most of those cameras, cash registers, etc.

The Antichrist's economic system will stop all commerce for those without the Mark. It will eventually behead most of them. This level of control will require a surveillance state like none before. It will require a police state that does not depend on the loyalty of individual officers. Antichrist's government will have to be totalitarian in order to coerce individuals to take the Mark or suffer the terrible consequences.

How Bad Could It Be?

Imagine a sky filled with high-tech drones. Imagine other drones walking and rolling along sidewalks, streets, through malls, warehouses, shopping centers, churches, schools, and office buildings. Imagine police prowl cars — both manned and unmanned — carrying more sensors than the Starship Enterprise.

Such machines will not only see the person. They will read the Mark and instantly know everything about him. They will flag anomalies as they look and listen inside homes and businesses. They will receive signals from personal smart devices such as cars, televisions, and phones. Even refrigerators and lamps will turn into informants for the new government. But for the sake of convenience and safety, it will seem worth it.

Robot police "dogs" are already at work in some law enforcement agencies. The Associated Press reports, "If you're homeless and looking for temporary shelter in Hawaii's capital, expect a visit from a robotic police dog that will scan your eye to make sure you don't have a fever."[92]

That might be okay if Spot is just checking for fever. But according to the AP, "Privacy watchdogs — the human kind — warn that police are secretly rushing to buy the robots without setting safeguards against aggressive, invasive or dehumanizing uses."[93]

Like the fictional "Terminator," a police drone, robot or any other AI based tool "can't be bargained with. It can't be reasoned with. It doesn't feel pity, or remorse, or fear. And it absolutely will not stop... ever."[94]

Could Dissenters Hide?

Imagine such machines used in a place where mildly criticizing the government is a crime — even in your own home. Every street corner camera, every passing telephone with its array of microphones, every police unit, and every drone will connect to a cloud database. Some probes will see and hear through walls. Hidden rooms will no longer be hidden. The Anne Franks and Corrie Ten Booms of the future will not have a chance.

Add to that a new wave of laws governing personal and seemingly minor aspects of life. Is your smart thermostat set too high in winter or too low in summer? Big brother will know. Of course, the end user might not control his thermostat. But if he

---

[92] "Robotic police dogs: Useful hounds or dehumanizing machines?" by Matt O'Brien and Jennifer Sinco Kelleher, the Associated Press, July 30, 2021

[93] Ibid.

[94] *The Terminator*, written by James Cameron and Gale Anne Hurd, Hemdale Film Corporation, 1984.

does, he had better set it in the correct range. This, they will say, can help us stay safe from the ravages of climate change.

The Bible says "lawlessness" will characterize the last days. As chaos rises, so will fear. Experiments in defunding police may simply lead to new names for the same job. But if carried far enough, it will mean crime waves with people demanding ever more police protection. "For your own safety," government will give law enforcement extraordinary new tools with which to "keep the peace."

Businesses already track us. A future government will be able to tap into that growing infrastructure of surveillance, even as it builds its own web of watching eyes connected to Artificial Intelligence. Businesses record and preserve our activities and proclivities. Your phone listens all the time, even when it is just standing by. Alexa® constantly waits for your next command. To make that possible, cloud-connected devices are always listening, always connected, and potentially sending every word you say... somewhere.

When Can Such Technology Be Built?

A system that puts every person in the world on a common grid is far more complex than a single chip. It takes a massive network of connections. H. G. Wells envisioned a "World Brain." Today, we have something very much like it. We call it "the world wide web."

The web has been worldwide since the early 1990s. But it still does not include everyone. The world's social planners consider internet access essential for the prosperity of nations and individuals. Several United Nations resolutions recognize internet access as a fundamental right.

PART SIX: BEAST WORLD

Ending internet disparity is the stated goal behind a flurry of activity by the United Nations, most first-world countries, global technology corporations, and the internet-impoverished third-world countries themselves. The world's governments and private enterprise are fully committed to the idea that every human on the face of the earth must be connected to the planet-wide grid.

That flurry of activity — infusing global technology with unprecedented amounts of money — is changing everything. The Mark of the Beast system is now under construction! Few of those developing it have any idea what they are building, how it will be used, or who it will ultimately serve. Nevertheless, it is happening. Much of the global network's hardware and software already exist. And the things still missing are on the drawing board.

Every one of us uses parts of that system every day — almost every minute.

Starlink and the New Constellations

When the Antichrist arrives on the global stage, he will find a full-blown technological infrastructure of astounding proportions already in operation. That infrastructure will have tentacles reaching into the life of every human being on earth. And it will await his use.

When I speak on this, most people want to know how the UN and others can wire every part of the earth. The answer is that they won't have to use wires.

Elon Musk's SpaceX plans to deploy what it calls a constellation of 42,000 Starlink satellites into Low Earth Orbit (LEO). These satellites alone will make broadband internet service available to virtually the entire planet. By May of 2022, SpaceX had already launched approximately 2,300 of the planned satellites.

Starlink has several well-heeled competitors. Amazon's Project Kuiper plans to create a global mesh of 3,276 satellites. OneWeb is a joint venture with Airbus. It expects to send at least 648 satellites into orbit. A Canadian telecommunications company, Telesat, has announced plans to place 298 satellites in an orbit twice as high as Starlink satellites. China has also announced plans to enter the race. Other countries and companies have hinted at similar plans.

You can see why astronomers complain about the clutter of low orbit satellites that have already begun to hamper their ability to use ground-based telescopes to study the heavens. In April of 2022, CNN reported, "In less than a decade, 1 out of every 15 points of light in the night sky will actually be a moving satellite."

And these are just the space-oriented internet providers. Earthbound plans are also underway to make the internet completely ubiquitous everywhere on the planet, and for every person. Not all will succeed, but the Mark of the Beast infrastructure will not need them all.

Access to the internet does not equal the Mark of the Beast. But a system of complete economic control must somehow link individuals on a global scale. For the first time in history, we can see the means of that connectivity.

PART SIX: BEAST WORLD

CHAPTER 21

Beast Money

During the Antichrist's heyday, every transaction will run through a grid connected to a global database. The system will remove money from the user's primary account, or any of the eligible accounts they choose. The user might be buying a used car from an individual, buying costume jewelry at a flea market, making a mortgage payment, or shopping online. The Mark will facilitate and monitor every sale and every purchase of every kind.

But you can't do that with cash.

What Will Happen to Cash?

The end of cash fits perfectly with Bible prophecy. Even those futurists who know nothing about end-times prophecy have concluded that cash is fast dying. Environmental fears, enhanced trade, calls for social justice, and even hygiene will all figure into the end of cash. Authorities see cash as not only inefficient, but also dangerous. It lacks the kind of minute-by-minute governmental control seen as crucial by the world's elite.

Globalists can point to a long list of potential benefits of going cashless. Terrorist funding will dry up. It will stymy other kinds of organized crime by putting a stop to money laundering. And it would make tax evasion far more difficult.

A few years ago, the issue of cash and germs was not a big deal. But we now have a newly minted generation of germophobes. To them, cash can be a health issue. In 2014, NPR ran the headline, "Dirty Money: A Microbial Jungle Thrives In Your Wallet."[95]

Jesus told us that in the last days, there wouldn't just be one global plague. He spoke of "plagues" — plural. Covid-19 will not be the end of plagues for this generation. New plagues will create new hysteria over possible agents of infection — like cash.

Big government does not like cash and neither does big business. Cash is hard to track and control. It can aid crime. It gives individuals a level of privacy that hinders the purposes of global corporations and would make a global government difficult to achieve.

What Will Replace Cash?

Future currency will be digital. But I'm not referring to private cryptocurrencies such as Bitcoin. I'm talking about government-backed digital currencies. At the 2022 World Government

---

[95] "Dirty Money: A Microbial Jungle Thrives In Your Wallet" by Michaeleen Doucleff, NPR, April 23, 2014.

PART SIX: BEAST WORLD

Summit in Dubai, American economist Dr. Pippa Malmgren explained the difference. "This new money will be sovereign in nature. Most people think that digital money is crypto, and private. But what I see are superpowers introducing digital currency. The Chinese were the first. The US is on the brink, I think, of moving in the same direction. The Europeans have committed to that as well."

To a large degree, currency has already gone digital. According to the trading app Invstr, "There are 180 different types of currencies in the world today. And incredibly, only 8% of it is actual, physical, hold-it-in-your-hand cash." Today's money mostly exists as zeroes and ones in a cyber-universe. Still, the system was originally built around cash, and cash remains at its heart. For those intent on control, that's a problem.

Private digital currencies use a technology called "blockchain." Blockchain is almost impossible to hack and highly decentralized, spread out on massive computing systems across the globe.

Governments see tremendous potential in blockchain technology. In 2021, China began rolling out the "digital yuan." CNBC's Dain Evans wrote, "China is beating the US when it comes to innovation in online money, posing challenges to the US dollar's status as the de facto monetary reserve. Nearly 100 countries — including China and the US — are developing a CBDC, or Central Bank Digital Currency. It's a form of money that's regulated but exists entirely online. China has already launched its digital yuan to more than a million Chinese citizens."[96]

---

[96] "China's digital yuan could pose challenges to the U.S. dollar" by Dain Evants, CNBC, July 24, 2021, Updated July 25, 2021, at 5:11 AM EDT.

One Money, One World

After government-controlled digital currencies become common, the obvious step will be to link them. This will promote international trade, help law enforcement, and stop currency manipulation. It will create trillions in corporate profits while allowing its proponents to signal their virtue by seeming to promote "equity."

Linking the currencies means the creation of a single standard. That standard will become the new coin of the global realm.

The US dollar has long stood as the world's reserve currency. That gives the United States several economic advantages. For instance, the US government borrows money at lower costs than other nations. Other nations do not like this. And many American leaders would like to end any practices that seem to put America first.

It would be difficult to overstate the significance of the financial revolution now taking place. Dr. Malmgren said it well. "What underpins a world order is always the financial system…. We are on the brink of a dramatic change where we are about to — and I'll say this boldly — we're about to abandon the traditional system of money and accounting, and introduce a new one. And the new one, the new accounting is what we call blockchain. It means digital, it means having an almost perfect record of every single transaction that happens in the economy."

For centuries, Christian scholars scratched their heads when they looked at scripture regarding a future where every monetary transaction must be authorized by a world governmental authority. They wondered what it could mean. A literal interpretation seemed absurd because they had no concept of such technology. And yet, in 2022, this globalist scholar seemed giddy about the implications of a technology that will give government "an almost perfect record of every single transaction that happens in the economy."

She was not talking about a city's economy or even a nation's economy. She was speaking to the World Government Summit. She included every single transaction — every bit of buying and selling — in the entire world.

Global money is the shortcut to global governance.

PART SIX: BEAST WORLD

CHAPTER 22

Why People Allow Government to Domination

Twenty years ago in the United States, this would have been a tough question. Back then, almost no American imagined the loss of rights and privacy we now consider routine. In the tribulation, loss of human rights will grow far, far worse. But the reasoning and habits that will make people feel they must relinquish their rights are already in place.

Reason # 1 — Peace and Safety

1 Thessalonians 5:3 warns, "When they say, 'Peace and safety!' then sudden destruction comes upon them, as labor pains upon a pregnant woman. And they shall not escape."

Jesus said the last days would be a time of pestilence,

lawlessness, and war.[97] To a generation raised on the idea that avoiding death is the primary purpose of life, the fear will be debilitating. In such a time, humanity will be willing — even longing — to exchange formerly precious things for the promise of "peace and safety."

People will feel they must choose between either Antichrist and his Mark, or economic and ecological ruin. Bear in mind that when we say, "economic ruin," we are not talking about a mere downturn in the markets or higher unemployment figures. We are talking about starvation, riots, marauding gangs seeking food and handing out street justice. Economic ruin means no more safety net, a collapsed healthcare system, and dozens of other ways in which civilization itself becomes broken and ineffective.

The fear will be so great that people and their governments will be willing to unify power in a single man. That is the world Antichrist will step into — a world not only ready for him — but craving him. They will hunger for his message, his attitudes, and even his totalitarian rules and political structures. He will convince them that they need his "strong regulations" (i.e., "tyrannical laws") in order to be safe. The scripture says the "safety" he gives will not last, but a panicked populous will not know that. Their desire for safety will catapult the Antichrist to power.

The Mark of the Beast system will promise new levels of medical safety. In times of increased lawlessness, it will promise security against crime. With the world convinced that climate change is an extinction-level problem, the Mark will promise an end to the climate crisis. Today, the fear of war has again come to mean the fear of nuclear annihilation. Unified rule will seem

---

[97] Luke 21:10-11, Matthew 24:12

to end that threat.

Finally, remember that "peace and safety" are not just carrots, but also sticks — not just promises, but threats. In the New World Order, those without the Mark will not be safe and will not live in peace.

Reason #2 — Convenience and Ease

Even if the Mark system cannot achieve its proponent's promises in its first iteration, they will be able to plausibly predict its role in a later fulfillment of their utopian dreams.

The Mark of the Beast system will promise to be the most convenient thing ever invented. Long lines at the airport would disappear — just breeze in and walk on to your plane. Think of how attractive that would be to the frequent fliers, as well as the once-a-year vacationer.

Imagine a trip to the doctor's office. No need to check in, the computer alerts office personnel before you walk in the door. Changes to your insurance instantly show up in the billing office. Has another doctor prescribed a change in medication? You don't have to tell the doctor. She sees it on a computer screen before she even sees you.

For diabetics, it might mean glucose monitoring without sticks in the fingers or the bulky continuous monitors now in use.

As I write this, several supermarkets including the Amazon-owned Whole Foods, have announced plans to have people pay for their groceries with a scan of their palms. But implanted chip technology might eliminate the palm scans. Think of going into a store, putting items in the shopping cart, and then walking out the door. No, you didn't just shoplift. The store automatically scanned the items on your way out the door. It scanned you, too. The computer then debits your bank account for the purchase. Easy-peasy.

Machines scanned you and watched you throughout the store. Intrusive? Maybe. But oh-so-convenient. Shoplifting will become impossible. Theoretically, that will bring down prices. Today, many jurisdictions no longer prosecute shoplifters. As a result, shoplifting has reached pandemic levels. This is destroying small businesses that can't afford to give away so much stuff. Big chain stores put more and more merchandise in locked glass cabinets. That will no longer be necessary with the Mark of the Beast.

Identity theft is both an inconvenience and a fundamental fear. The world is already desperate for a solution, but the problem keeps getting worse. Present systems are faltering under the load. IDs and instruments of credit can be forged or hacked. But the Mark of the Beast system will promise rock solid security when it comes to your identity, your property, and your information.

Are you concerned about election fraud or suppression of the vote? The Beast system will promise a quick and emphatic end to both concerns.

Does it get your goat that while you pay your full share of taxes, others get away with cheating? In a system with complete government monitoring of all transactions, cheating on taxes at all levels will end. But at the same time, getting every deduction will be automatic. Imagine a world where doing taxes is a snap. It may never be that easy, but those are the kinds of promises the Mark's proponents will make.

PART SIX: BEAST WORLD

Reason #3 — Financial Rescue and the Promise of Prosperity

As mentioned earlier, it would take a complete global economic collapse or the imminent threat of such a collapse to compel world leaders to relinquish control of money. Bible prophecies tell us about more than one such collapse during the tribulation. Like so many things that prophecy teaches about those seven years, we see the groundwork being laid now — primarily in the form of deficit spending at fantastic levels. This phenomenon is not isolated to a few nations. It threatens the economies of every nation on earth.

The old saying goes, "When your outgo exceeds your income, your upkeep will be your downfall." Governments everywhere now spend far more than they bring in. I could give hundreds of examples of their profligate spending models. But you already know them. The pace of worldwide deficit spending staggers the mind, and it keeps getting worse.

Covid-related spending brought the world's economies to the brink of bankruptcy. But as global emergencies go, Covid was mild. What would a more severe problem do? During the tribulation, global disasters will be the order of the day. Even national leaders do not survive this level of turmoil.

And when the crisis is planetwide, nations will not be able to bail one another out. They will all be failing at once. Who will rescue the nations when even the US economy is crippled? A global economic meltdown in our time would be like nothing seen before.

MARKING THE MASSES

PART SIX: BEAST WORLD

CHAPTER 23

Super Capacities

"Now all of us can talk to the NSA — just by dialing any number."

— *David Letterman.*

Consider eight billion people having all their activities logged and stored. Think of the data created by phone calls, internet traffic, sales, conversations held near connected devices, images taken near connected cameras. This includes images from an enormous network of street cameras and microphones, law enforcement drones and police vehicles, satellites, business communications, and on and on.

Imagine a world where government routinely stores just about everything on just about everyone. That volume of data raises two crucial questions. 1- Could even a global government store that much data? 2- How could that government make sense of so much data?

How Can So Much Data Be Stored?

Digital storage is cheap. Brewster Kahle founded the Internet Archive and Alexa Internet (later sold to Amazon). He said, "If one had the opportunity to collect all the voice traffic in the US it would cost less than the Pentagon spends on paperclips. Storage these days is trivial, it's not a problem."

In 2019, the Kingston company announced the deployment of a 4-terabyte thumb drive. To visualize that, imagine plain text data printed on letter size sheets of paper single-spaced with a 12-point font and one-inch margins. We can store written data at a rate of 500 pages per megabyte. With 20-pound stock laid flat, 500 sheets rise 2 ½ inches — so, one megabyte of digital storage equals 2 ½ inches of paper filled with words.

A terabyte is a million times larger than a megabyte. Four terabytes are four million times larger. That means a thumb drive can now hold the equivalent of a stack of paper 158 miles high. In July of 2021, a New Shepherd rocket blasted owner Jeff Bezos and his passengers about 50 miles into the sky. The media called it "the edge of space." A thumb drive can now hold the equivalent of a stack of paper more than three times that high.

According to a 2013 article in Forbes, "You would need just 400 terabytes to hold all of the books ever written in any language."[98] In other words, 100 of the tiny thumb drives could hold all the books ever written as of 2013. Add in the books written since then, and you could still toss it all into a small

---

[98] "Blueprints Of NSA's Ridiculously Expensive Data Center In Utah Suggest It Holds Less Info Than Thought" by Kashmir Hill, Forbes, July 24, 2013.

shoebox.

If modern technology allows us to put that amount of data in such a small space, what can the NSA do with hundreds of thousands of square feet?

The Mark of the Beast system will need central processing centers of almost unthinkable power and scope. Here's the stunning thing. Governments and mega-corporations are building those processing centers right now. <u>In May of 2014, the NSA opened the Utah Data Center.</u> The facility covers a million square feet. Electricity costs are estimated at $40 million a year. The facility uses four 25,000 square foot buildings to store data — a lot of shoeboxes.

Most of the center's capabilities are classified. However, the MITRE Corporation, a Pentagon think tank, estimated that the facility can hold "yottabytes" of data. *Wired Magazine* published the same thing — "yottabytes." Most experts believe the number is lower than that. Still, it's staggering to think that both of these respected organizations would arrive at such a fantastic guess.

Unless you are a computer geek, you may not have heard the word "<u>yottabyte</u>." A yottabyte is <u>a trillion times larger than a</u> terabyte. If we printed a yottabyte of plain text on paper and laid each page flat, the stack of paper would rise 39.5 billion miles. For reference, Pluto orbits at 3.7 billion miles from the sun. Our stack of paper would go far outside our solar system.

Is that amount of digital data storage even possible in four buildings that are each a little larger than a Walmart® Superstore? Experts disagree. But whatever its capacity, the Utah Center is not alone. The data storage buildings at the NSA's Texas Cryptology Center near San Antonio have a footprint two and a half times that of the facility in Utah.

We do not know the capability of the NSA's Fort Meade headquarters in Maryland. However, government reports show that they already use more electricity than the new Utah Center. Massive use of electricity usually means massive amounts of computing power. We know that in 2009, the NSA placed in the Federal Register a 20-year plan to build 5.8 million square feet of new working and storage space at Fort Meade.

These facilities represent one agency in one nation. Add to that the other governments of the world. Then add in the massive Google servers and the Amazon servers and all the rest of the private sector. After all, a totalitarian regime feels no compunction about crossing the line between private enterprise and government. It commandeers what it wants.

While serving as the CIA's Chief Technology Officer, Gus Hunt explained the US intelligence community's data strategy. He said, "We fundamentally try to collect everything and hang on to it forever." "Everything" and "forever" are very big words.

In that same speech, he said, "It is really very nearly within our grasp to be able to compute on all human generated information." He said those words in 2013 — eons ago in terms of technological advances.

Storage of the data will not be a problem.

How Can Anyone Make Sense of So Much Data?

There are not enough people to work through the vast amount of data already available. But the rise of Artificial Intelligence (AI) changes everything. AI will sort the data and draw conclusions.

PART SIX: BEAST WORLD

Artificial Intelligence is not intelligent in a human sense. It has no self-awareness, no consciousness. <u>It will draw conclusions based on its programming</u>. If programmers decide that going to church is a suspicious activity, it will pay special attention to churchgoers.

Programmers will build the algorithms allowing computers to correlate the world's data. A computer will decide whether someone uses too much water or buys more gas than they should. AI programs can already read a person's mood by examining facial expressions and body language. Law enforcement strategists believe they will soon be able to tell when someone plans to commit a robbery. It will not be completely accurate, but the new society will consider false pre-arrests part of the price for "peace and safety."

In the Summer of 2021, the Pentagon announced a series of tests called the Global Information Dominance Experiments. They believe they can use AI in conjunction with their amazing information gathering abilities to see the battlefield "days in advance." In other words, they think AI will soon allow them to see the future.

The Mark of the Beast will make it possible for AI to link and correlate the vast data that already exists about every person in the world. It will connect the old data to a tsunami of new information related to buying, selling, and loyal worship of the "dear leader."

Think the power and application of AI for a one world government and the Mark of the Beast still sounds like science fiction? As hard as it is to believe, it's not. Its abilities are already here, and you can interact with it right now!

ChatGPT

For years, the world of technology has been buzzing about AI, but with the advent in 2022 of something called ChatGPT, interest in AI has exploded. People who never thought it possible to lose their jobs to automation, are suddenly scared. This could be the first salvo in a revolution that radically changes everything for humanity.

Few people realize the significance of Artificial Intelligence to Bible prophecy. These programs are already being used as some of the most powerful tools of oppression the world has ever seen. For instance, they lie at the heart of China's social credit system. And they're just getting started!

ChatGPT is the fastest growing app of all time, gaining 100 million active users within two months of its release. It took TikTok nine months to get that many users.

There's a free version of ChatGPT, but the goal is to make money. The owners of the product, a company called OpenAI, will license the technology to other companies for a fee. For instance, Microsoft is integrating the technology into its web browser, Edge, and into its search engine, Bing. Microsoft also owns a sizeable stake in OpenAI.

When a ZDNet reporter asked ChatGPT if it is "the fastest growing app in history?" the program answered that it is not an app at all. It called itself "a machine learning model designed to generate human-like text based on the input provided to it."

A program generating "human-like text" is the primary reason ChatGPT is getting so much attention in the press. Tell it to write a 1,000-word essay on the creation of the Panama Canal and, within seconds, you've got a 1,000-word essay on the creation of the Panama Canal. This has the world's journalists scared. After all, it does what they do, only faster and cheaper. This thing seems to be gunning for their jobs. OpenAI warns that their product may include inaccurate data, but, unfortunately, human journalists exhibit the same tendency.

The Creation Becomes the Creator

ChatGPT can also write computer programs and build websites. This is the beginning of the era when <u>machines will be the primary programmers of other machines</u>.

It's not just reporters and programmers who could be made obsolete by the new technology. AI will soon be able to pass bar exams in all states. Whether diminishing the number of lawyers is good or bad may be up for debate, but it has them scared. ChatGPT recently passed the US Medical Licensing Examination. That doesn't mean it can now serve as a doctor, but we're headed that way.

This hits close to home. These programs are already being used to write sermons, and they will soon be able to create their own handsome human simulations to deliver those sermons in any style a congregation might want. Maybe a church might decide they would like to hear a Billy Graham-style preacher every week rather than the all-too-human pastor they're stuck with now.

There are A.I.s on the drawing board that would replace almost every human in the making of motion pictures. That includes replacing the actors — in some cases replacing them with actors who died fifty years ago. They can create music, landscapes, and "people" from scratch.

Marking the Masses

In fact, to drive the point home, the cover art for the very book you're reading was generated entirely by AI. It's difficult to wrap one's head around this, but the cover you see was not derived or modified from existing images on the web from other various human artists, but is entirely original artwork generated by artificial intelligence in about 30 second through utilizing massive amounts of cloud-based processing.

What question did my publishing company ask AI in order to generate this cover? They asked, "show me what the New World Order might look like." If this doesn't send shivers down your spine, I'm not sure what will.

AI right now has some positive aspects for research and work applications; however, this very tool can also easily "read" every online book in the world to immediately determine if there's content that's against the social guidelines of a government or retailer – banning the books in question instantly. With speech recognition, it can "listen" to every sermon, every interview and every statement spoken by anyone on a social media platform and immediately know if your opinions or statement should be banned or flagged as dangerous or hateful.

Are you a Republican? A Democrat? Are you anti-LGBTQ+? Are you a Christian? AI will be able to determine this in a matter of seconds based on your online posts, photos, personal texts and videos and purchases!

AI will become the ultimate tool to enforce global compliance.

PART SIX: BEAST WORLD

The Image of the Beast

In Revelation 13:15, the Bible seems to be giving us a picture of an AI machine replicating human thought and speech. "He [the Antichrist's cohort known as the False Prophet] was granted power to give breath to the image of the beast, that the image of the beast should both speak and cause as many as would not worship the image of the beast to be killed."

This might be fulfilled by something as simple as a television image, but I don't think so. It talks about this image being a point of worship, like King Nebuchadnezzar's image that Shadrach, Meshach, and Abednego refused to worship in ancient Babylon. Television images of a world leader seem too ordinary to invoke worship.

The image also speaks. Again, it could just be a recorded voice, but I think AI is more likely. Notice that "the image of the beast" will "cause as many as would not worship the image of the beast to be killed." It enforces its own worship! This implies thought, control, and verbal interaction with people — not something prerecorded, but something programmed to simulate a thinking entity.

The very next verses talk about the Mark of the Beast economic system, implying that this Artificial Intelligence helps to promote and facilitate the 6-6-6 system.

In the days of Antichrist, AI computers will monitor the world's financial transactions and will have armies of AI robots to enforce the rules. This will allow an incredibly small portion of the population to control everyone else. And, ultimately, this is about control — not convenience, not creativity, not democracy — but control.

Growing Deception

ChatGPT is just a drop of water in the sea of new technologies. There are already hundreds, if not thousands, of various AI-powered tools that have been released as of May 2023 that are being integrated into everything from your smart phone to your vehicle — likely without you even knowing it. As unsettling as tools like ChatGPT are, they are almost elementary in comparison to other terrifying technologies already being utilized by some of the largest companies and governments on the planet — such as quantum computing —but that's a topic for another time. This clearly foreshadows the ability how a few people can control access to information for billions. In Matthew 24, Jesus repeatedly warns that the time approaching His return would be filled with deception. We see the same idea in other parts of the New Testament, and it will include what we might call, "church people."

2 Timothy 4:3-4 warns, "The time will come when they will not endure sound doctrine, but according to their own desires, because they have itching ears, they will heap up for themselves teachers; and they will turn their ears away from the truth, and be turned aside to fables."

We have already entered a time when wrong doctrine, fake news, false prophecy, and dishonest science have taken over much of the church establishment around the world.

This will only get worse.

PART SIX: BEAST WORLD

Always Watching

Machines already monitor our every drive, every walk, most of our transactions, the television programs we watch, our internet searches, medical treatments, the clothes we wear, whether or not we floss, bank deposits and withdrawals, food purchases (including the amount of fat and sugar we consume), water use, electricity use, and just about every other aspect of life. The difference is that the Mark of the Beast system will centralize all the data and use its Artificial Intelligence to correlate that data and draw conclusions.

PART SEVEN

Hope and Victory

MARKING THE MASSES

PART SEVEN: HOPE AND VICTORY

CHAPTER 24

Tipping Point

Children sing, "I'm a little teapot, Short and stout... Tip me over and pour me out."

Liquid obeys its master — gravity. It flows where gravity takes it. Contained by the sides, floor, and ceiling of the pot, steeping tea merely rests. But tip it over and the spout shows its purpose — the controlled, gentle, and beneficial outflow of liquid.

Though essential for life and pleasant in hundreds of ways, water can also be dangerous. Water exploding through a crumbling dam destroys buildings, drowns people, and rearranges the terrain along its path. Flood water is startling in its power. It destroys crops, flattens trees, moves buses and trucks. With deafening violence, it takes houses off their foundations and turns lovingly sculpted structures into rubble.

Tsunami victims often tell the story of an unexpected effect. The water's movement is so powerful, it rips away their clothes. But modesty is the least among their worries. The heaving, lunging force of the water also shatters bones, shoves them where they don't want to go, cuts off their air, and fills their lungs with death.

We stand beneath the long leaky dam of human civilization. We've been watching the cracks grow as the years have passed. Occasional breaks have taken place, breaks that threatened the integrity of the dam as a whole. But a strong underlying structure allowed us to make at least temporary repairs. Good men and women stuck their fingers in the dyke, and it seemed to hold.

But the breaches keep growing. They have long since become too big for small fingers. The reservoir of power on the other side leaks through and sometimes gushes forth in ever more dangerous ways. It presses for release. A torrent of death waits above our heads.

<u>According to the Bible, a tipping point will come, and human edifices against lawlessness and evil will finally fall flat.</u> Today, we see the dam up the hill breaking before our eyes. An unfathomably large flood awaits that fall. It will search out low ground, and it will find it everywhere. We stand in the flood's path. The dam begins to break.

Are we doomed? We don't have to be. Is there anything we can do to help ourselves, our loved ones, and others? Yes. This book has been about the direction of the flow of destruction now deluging our world. That destruction is following a path mapped out by the Bible thousands of years ago.

But the Bible is not primarily about destruction. Most of all, the Bible is a book about redemption. That includes instructions on staying safe in troubled times, and, often, how to avoid the trouble entirely.

A vicious, new world order roars down upon us. But before we panic, we need to understand that God told us about it in incredible detail long ago. And, despite the tendency to be enraged or terrorized by the events of our time, <u>God still says to</u> each of us, "<u>Fear not!</u>"

Can the Horrors of the Mark Be Avoided?

1 Corinthians 15:51 makes a startling announcement. "Behold, I tell you a mystery: We shall not all sleep, but we shall all be changed."

Jesus and others in the New Testament often referred to death as "sleep." That word is a statement of faith in the fact of resurrection. Jesus taught that He would raise His followers from the dead. In John 11:25, He said, "I am the resurrection and the life. He who believes in Me, though he may die, he shall live."

At the point of the rapture, Christ will physically raise from the dead all who have died in Him. He will give them new, immortal bodies.

What about those who are in Christ, but have not died? Will the believers who are still alive at the moment of the resurrection, miss out? No. 1 Thessalonians 4:16-17 says, "The dead in Christ will rise first. Then we who are alive and remain shall be caught up together with them in the clouds to meet the Lord in the air."

The dried-up old mortal bodies of the dead will change into stupendous new resurrection bodies as they rise from their graves. Then, those who are in Christ but still living will change. They will go from <u>mortal to immortal in the blink of an eye</u>.

> *Behold, I tell you a mystery: We shall not all sleep, but we shall all be changed — in a moment, in the twinkling of an eye, at the last trumpet. For the trumpet will sound, and the dead will be raised incorruptible, and we shall be changed. For this corruptible must put on incorruption, and this mortal must put on immortality.*
> *— 1 Corinthians 15:51-53*

Living believers will get resurrection bodies without being raised from the dead because they will never have died. Both groups will rise to meet the Lord in the air. This is the rapture, the blessed hope of all Christians. We may differ on the details, but we agree that a bodily resurrection is coming — a resurrection like that of the Lord.

I am completely convinced that the rapture will take place before the tribulation.[99] Those who come to Christ before the rapture will avoid the Mark of the Beast and the other awful events prophesied for that time.

Should Christians Be Concerned?

Followers of Christ need not fret over personally facing the Mark of the Beast. But love requires our concern for others. Knowing the agonies of the tribulation should encourage all who know Jesus to get the Gospel out as fast and effectively as we can.

Those who miss the rapture but later turn to Christ, will be

---

[99] In another Define series book, I plan to give details about the Bible's clear teaching that the rapture takes place before the tribulation.

left in a world of torture and pain. But in the end, things will be far worse for those who refuse Christ and receive the Mark. They will have eternally rejected God from their lives. They will have stepped past the line of possible salvation. And that is a big, big deal!

Dismal as some of this can be, it should also bring strong encouragement to those who have trusted their lives to Christ. It proves yet again the Bible's reliability. With our own eyes, we see the world rushing madly toward the Mark of the Beast — a concept unfathomable to earlier generations. Then we remember that the Book of Revelation was written more than 1,900 years ago.

How Can I Be Sure I Am Ready?

Do you want to be sure that when you die, you will go to heaven? Do you want to be certain what will happen to you when the trumpet sounds, and Jesus calls His people into the sky? Those two questions boil down to the same thing. As a friend of mine says, "If you're ready to die, you're ready to fly."

But are you truly ready? If not, the time to do so is right now — not later today or sometime tomorrow. *Right now*. 2 Corinthians 6:2 says, "This is the hour to receive God's favor; today is the day to be saved!"[100]

We've discussed throughout this book how global deception is clearly upon us, and how that deception has penetrated the hearts and minds of many within the church. As we rapidly

---

[100] Scripture quotation is from the *Good News Translation in Today's English Version*- Second Edition Copyright © 1992 by American Bible Society. Used by Permission.

approach the end of the age, it's critical to understand that proclaiming that Jesus Christ is the Son of God isn't the same thing as receiving Him as your Lord and Savior. After all, James 2:19 tells us that even the demons believe that Jesus is the Son of God… and tremble.

In the matter of saving faith, the more important and often marginalized question is that if we must believe into the Lord Jesus Christ to be saved, then what does Jesus define as belief? It's a question that more church goers today should be seeking to answer, and a critical topic in these times of deception that pastors should be proactively teaching their congregations.

Believing in Jesus is more than a conscious acknowledgment of who He is and what He has done. More specifically, Romans 10:9 tells us that you must also "believe in your heart" and Jesus provided numerous parables and examples to clarify what this means. Through your trust in Jesus, He will put your old self to death, and the evidence that this transition took place is reflected by the change in your life. This is what it means to be "born again".

The very question of clarity regarding how one may receive salvation was asked by a Pharisee named Nicodemus who met with Jesus in secret. Jesus provided Nicodemus an answer that we should all be familiar with, but few dwell upon.

> *Jesus answered, "Most assuredly, I say to you, unless one is born of water and the Spirit, he cannot enter the kingdom of God. That which is born of the flesh is flesh, and that which is born of the Spirit is spirit. Do not marvel that I said to you, 'You must be born again.'*
> *— John 3:5-7*

PART SEVEN: HOPE AND VICTORY

Being born again is not a symbolic acknowledgement of faith, but a literal transformation from our old self into a new creation in Christ, which only through Him dwelling within us, frees us from the bondage of sin. A transformation that leads us to walk in righteousness and be a light in the world. Salvation comes from God. So, ask Him for it. You will be asking for a gift He longs to give you. 2 Peter 3:9 says that He is "not willing that any should perish but that all should come to repentance."

Until that day the Lord returns for His faithful, I pray that His peace will provide comfort beyond all understanding through the storms of this life and may the armor of God protect and strengthen you to endure until the end.

"Then they will deliver you up to tribulation and kill you, and you will be hated by all nations for My name's sake. And then many will be offended, will betray one another, and will hate one another. Then many false prophets will rise up and deceive many. And because lawlessness will abound, the love of many will grow cold. But he who endures to the end shall be saved."

— Matthew 24:9-13